SOFTWARE GUIDE

Using VP-Planner Plus

Ernest S. Colantonio

University of Illinois

D. C. HEATH AND COMPANY

Lexington, Massachusetts Toronto

Photo Credits

Figures 1.2, 1.3, 1.7, and 1.8(d) courtesy of International Business Machines Corp.
Figure 1.4 courtesy of Intel.
Figure 1.5 courtesy of Memorex.
Figure 1.6 courtesy of Seagate Technologies.
Figures 1.10(b) and 1.11 courtesy of Hewlett Packard.

Published simultaneously in Canada.

Printed in the United States of America.

International Standard Book Number: 0-669-19958-3

10 9 8 7 6 5 4 3 2

Preface

In this day and age, it's become increasingly evident that a truly general education must include some exposure to computers. Fortunately, microcomputers have become so inexpensive that literally millions of them have surfaced in homes, schools, offices, and businesses everywhere. What's more, they're being used by people from all walks of life. For most of us, being able to use a computer for daily tasks means learning to use prewritten software. Although there are thousands of different programs available for every conceivable purpose, operating systems and spreadsheet packages stand out as two of the most important. Being able to use these types of software is quickly becoming essential for students, professionals, and home users.

The Purpose of This Guide

This guide can be used in any introductory class that teaches the use of these two specific types of software:

1. IBM PC-DOS or MS-DOS
2. VP-Planner Plus

Its lessons teach the student, in a hands-on, step-by-step approach, how to apply these programs to common tasks. For the greatest understanding, students should follow the manual as they run the software on their own (or their school's or employer's) computer. On completion of the lessons, the student will be amply prepared to use each of these types of software for common applications.

The Software

The *Software Guide* teaches the use of the world's most popular microcomputer operating system, along with a highly regarded spreadsheet program. Although PC-DOS or MS-DOS is not included with this guide, a copy of this operating system is usually purchased as standard equipment with most IBM and IBM-compatible microcomputers. The most recent educational version of VP-Planner Plus is available with this guide.

PC-DOS and MS-DOS 3.30

Almost identical, these twins are the *de facto* standard operating system used on the IBM family of personal computers and compatible machines. Since everyone who uses one of these computers must deal with the operating system to some extent, DOS tops the list of important software to become familiar with. Most of the DOS commands covered in this guide also work with all versions of DOS 2.00 and higher, including IBM DOS 4.00.

VP-Planner Plus

VP-Planner Plus, from Paperback Software, replicates all of the features of Lotus 1-2-3, the best-selling application software package of all time. This program also offers features that surpass 1-2-3 in a number of areas. It not only has one of the most powerful spreadsheets in the business, VP-Planner Plus also includes graphics and data management capabilities.

VP-Planner Plus Features

- Makes full use of the IBM keyboard to allow easy movement to any position in a worksheet
- Allows labels, numbers, and formulas to be entered into a worksheet
- Allows existing worksheet data to be edited, modified, or updated
- Includes an excellent system of menus for selecting commands and options
- Includes a context-sensitive help facility
- Has an extensive array of formatting options
- Allows worksheets to be saved and retrieved from disks
- Generates printed reports
- Makes use of formulas to compute values
- Includes a rich set of built-in functions for use in formulas
- Has a keyboard macro facility
- Includes graphics capability
- Prints graphics from within the main program
- Has a data management capability

System Requirements

The following system requirements are needed to use this popular software:

- An IBM or IBM-compatible microcomputer
- MS- or PC-DOS Version 2.00 or higher
- At least 256K RAM
- An 80-column monochrome or color monitor
- A dot-matrix or laser printer
- Two 5¼-inch or 3½-inch floppy disk drives, or at least one floppy disk drive and a hard disk drive

The Guide

The *Software Guide* is both a user's manual and a workbook with exercises. It is specifically designed to be used with the software described above. This guide, which consists of three parts, covers:

1. An introduction to microcomputers
2. DOS instructions and exercises
3. VP-Planner Plus instructions and exercises

As a user's manual, the *Software Guide* provides an introduction to the specific type of software, a description of its general features, and a series of lessons on how to use these features. As a workbook, the *Software Guide* gives students clear explanations, step-by-step instructions, and plenty of exercises to practice and test their skills. More specifically, it includes:

- Clear learning objectives for each part
- A description of the software's general capabilities
- Carefully paced step-by-step lessons
- Over 150 exercises ranging in difficulty from simple to complex
- Numerous examples

- Answers to multiple choice and fill-in exercises
- Command summaries for DOS and VP-Planner Plus for easy reference
- A comprehensive glossary
- Exceptionally clear, actual screen views

The *Software Guide* can be assigned in class or used in a self-paced lab setting. Either way, the workbook will help students get the software experience they'll need in today's world.

Limitations of the Educational Version of VP-Planner Plus

The educational version of VP-Planner Plus is restricted to 64 columns (A through BL) and 256 rows (1 through 256). The Multidimensional Database feature is not included. VGA and ATI Wonder video card support has been removed.

There is approximately 32K space available for any sample files that the author may want to include on this disk. Note that the educational version of VP-Planner Plus requires at least 384K memory.

Acknowledgments

Several people were involved in making this project possible. I am especially grateful to Lee Ripley and Pam Kirshen for the inception of the idea for this manual's predecessors. Their help and support, along with that of Jill Hobbs, was greatly appreciated. Special thanks go to C. Brian Honess of the University of South Carolina for many of the short and long problems which were adapted from the original *Software Guide*. I'd like to thank Peter Gordon of D. C. Heath for his new vision of what these manuals could become, and Kitty Sheehan and Kathy Savage for handling all of those little details, as well as Cia Boynton, Janice Molloy, and Irene Cinelli for all the time and effort they contributed toward the completion of this project.

E. S. C.

Contents

1

The Microcomputer

Learning Objectives

After reading this chapter, you should know the following:

- What is meant by the term *microcomputer*
- The basic operations performed by all computers
- The four major hardware components of a typical microcomputer system
- The major components inside a microcomputer's system unit
- The three major types of microcomputer displays
- How the various special-purpose keys on a microcomputer keyboard are used
- The four most popular types of microcomputer printers
- The three major categories of microcomputer software
- How to turn on a microcomputer
- How to operate a microcomputer printer
- How to care for floppy disks

Introduction

We begin this first chapter by introducing IBM and IBM-compatible microcomputers, their hardware components, and popular types of software. (By *IBM-compatible* we mean any computer that works like a comparable IBM model and can run the same software.) Then we discuss a few helpful hints for working with microcomputers.

What Is a Microcomputer?

Its very name tells us that a **microcomputer** is a small computer, and a **computer** is an electronic device that performs calculations and processes data. Most people think of a microcomputer as being small enough to fit on top of a desk. Although some powerful models can serve several users simultaneously, most microcomputers are used by only one person at a time. For this reason, microcomputers are also often called **personal computers**.

Another characteristic of microcomputers is that their "brain" or **central processing unit (CPU)** consists of a single electronic device known as a **microprocessor**. This device, a marvel of miniature engineering, controls the microcomputer, performs its calculations, and processes data. A microprocessor is just one type of integrated circuit chip, which is a thin slice of semiconductor material, such as pure silicon crystal, impregnated with carefully selected impurities. These chips are commonly used in computers and many other modern electronic devices.

One way to define microcomputers is by what they do. They can be used to help accomplish many different tasks. At the lowest level, however, a microcomputer performs the same basic operations as all computers. This can be summed up as *input, processing*, and *output* (see Figure 1.1).

Figure 1.1 What a Computer Does

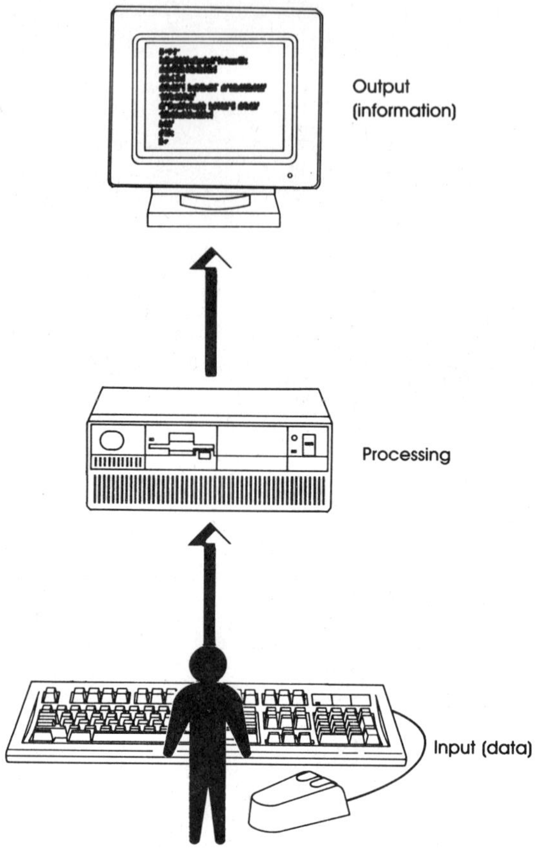

First, a **program** is needed to tell the computer what to do. This is a set of instructions that controls a computer's operation. The program lets you enter raw **data,** which can consist of numbers, text, pictures, and even sounds. These data entered into the computer are called **input**. The program instructs the computer to process the data by doing calculations, comparisons, and other manipulations. The final result is processed data or **information**, hopefully a more organized and useful form of the original input. This information produced by the computer is called **output**. Keep in mind that there is no magic here—a program is needed to tell the computer what to do and the output information is only as valid as the original input data.

Although microcomputers perform the same basic operations as larger computers, they differ in speed and capacity. Larger computers can generally process data faster than microcomputers. They can also internally store more data at a time than microcomputers. These factors make larger computers better for performing lots of extremely complex and time-consuming computations. Microcomputers are also less adept than larger computers at handling several different users or tasks at the same time. On the other hand, microcomputers are superbly adapted to help with many work-a-day tasks like typing papers, figuring taxes, maintaining mailing lists, sending messages, drawing charts, managing finances, and even playing games.

Finally, microcomputers generally fall within a given price range. This range varies from little as $100 to as much as $15,000. Today the average price of a typical microcomputer used in business is around $2500. This is, however, a good deal less than the cost of much more powerful computers, which may run into many thousands or millions of dollars. Although microcomputers are by no means cheap, their prices have been generally dropping even as their capabilities have increased. For example, in late 1983 the list price of a basic IBM Personal Computer XT was $5675. The list price of its successor, a similarly-equipped IBM Personal System/2 Model 30, was only $2545 when first released in mid 1987. Even though the newer Model 30 costs less than half as much as the old XT, it still has more than twice the speed and storage capacity, along with many other improvements.

Hardware

The **hardware** of a computer system is the electronic and mechanical equipment that make it work. Like a stereo system, microcomputer hardware generally consists of several distinct components connected by cables. Although there are several possible arrangements and many different models, Figure 1.2 shows a typical microcomputer system, the IBM Personal System/2 Model 50, which has four major parts: a system unit, display, keyboard, and printer. You will also notice, in this figure, a power switch, a floppy disk drive, and a mouse, all of which will be discussed later.

Figure 1.2 A Microcomputer System

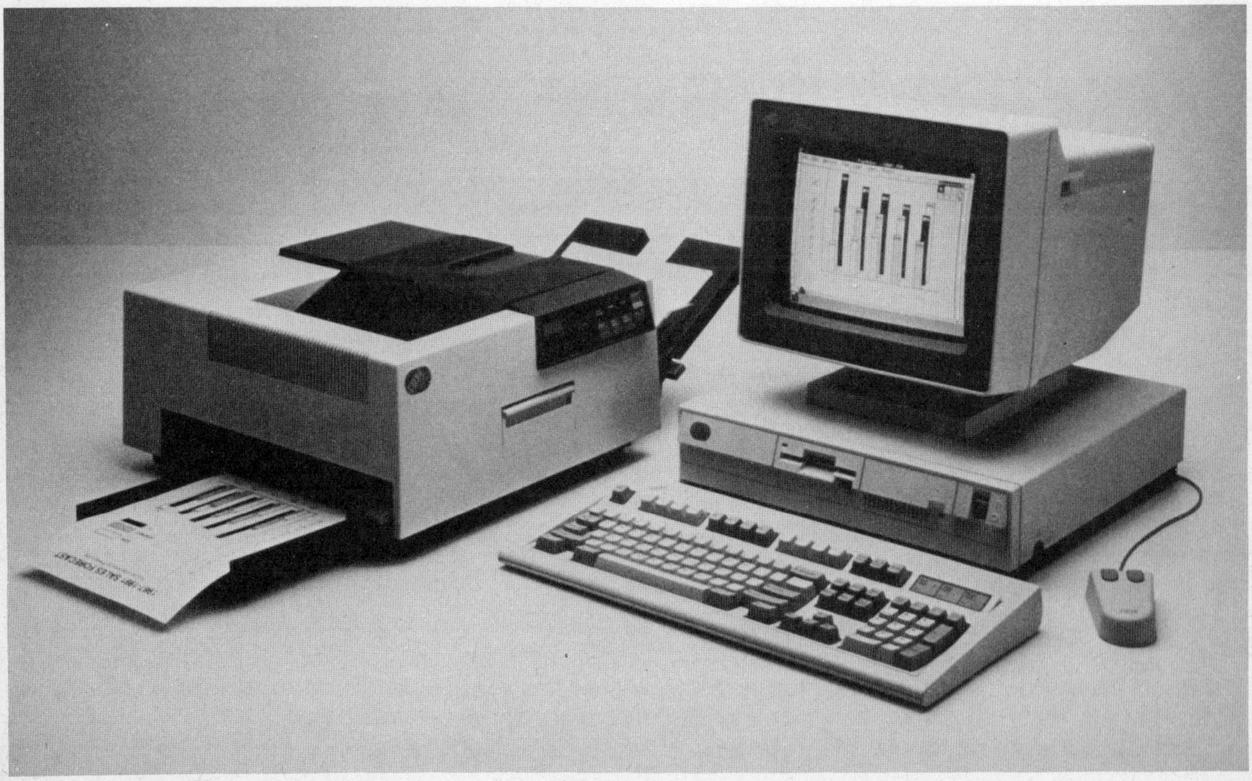

System Unit

From the outside, the system unit looks like a shallow box about the size of a portable typewriter. Figure 1.3 shows what the system unit of an IBM Personal System/2 Model 50 looks like on the inside. This central component houses important elements such as the computer's motherboard, microprocessor, memory, disk drives, and power supply.

Figure 1.3 Inside the System Unit

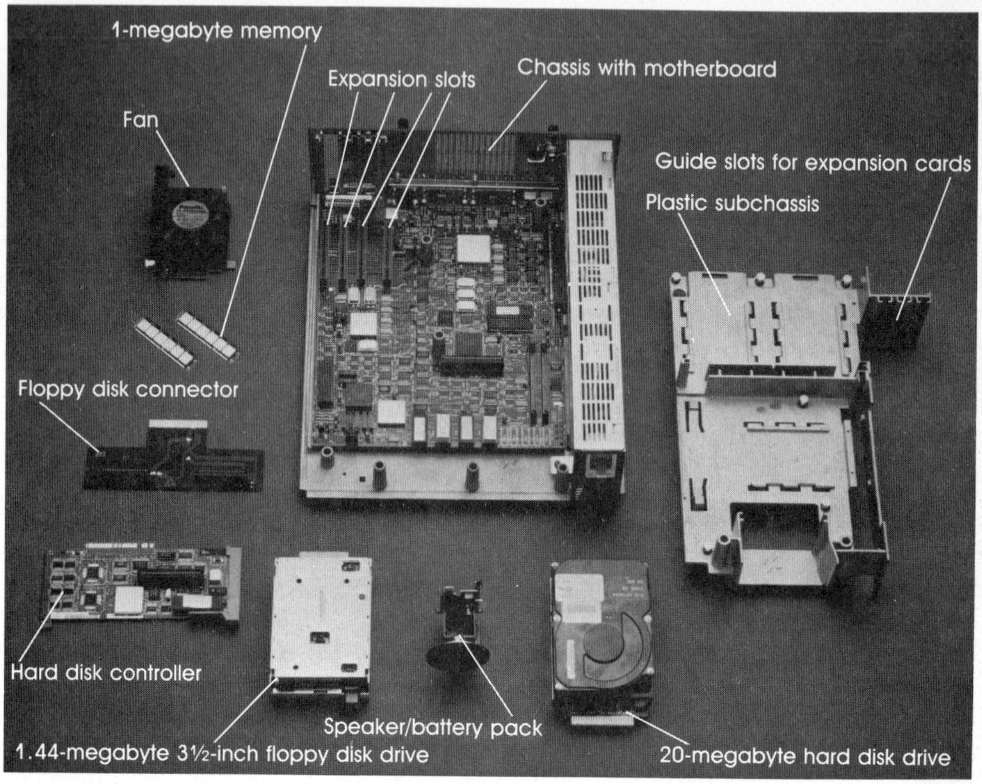

Motherboard

The main circuit board of a computer is called the **motherboard** or **system board** (see Figure 1.4). Among other components, the motherboard holds the computer's CPU, some memory, and much of its control circuitry. In addition, the motherboard contains the **bus**, a set of wires and connectors that link the CPU to memory and other computer components.

In most microcomputers, the bus is accessible through a series of **expansion slots**. Each expansion slot is an internal connector that allows you to plug an additional circuit board into the motherboard. The IBM Personal System/2 Model 50, for example, has four expansion slots, which can be seen in Figure 1.4. Some computers come with eight or more expansion slots. A circuit board that plugs into an expansion slot is called an **expansion board**, **card**, or **adapter**. Such circuit boards make it possible to connect a wide variety of extra equipment to a computer, thus *expanding* its capability.

The motherboard or expansion boards also contain device controllers. A **device controller** is a set of chips or a circuit board that operates a piece of computer equipment such as a disk drive, display, keyboard, mouse, or printer. Recently, there has been a trend toward building device controllers onto microcomputer motherboards. The IBM Personal System/2 Model 50 shown in Figure 1.4, for example, has most of its device controllers on the motherboard.

Figure 1.4
A Motherboard or System Board

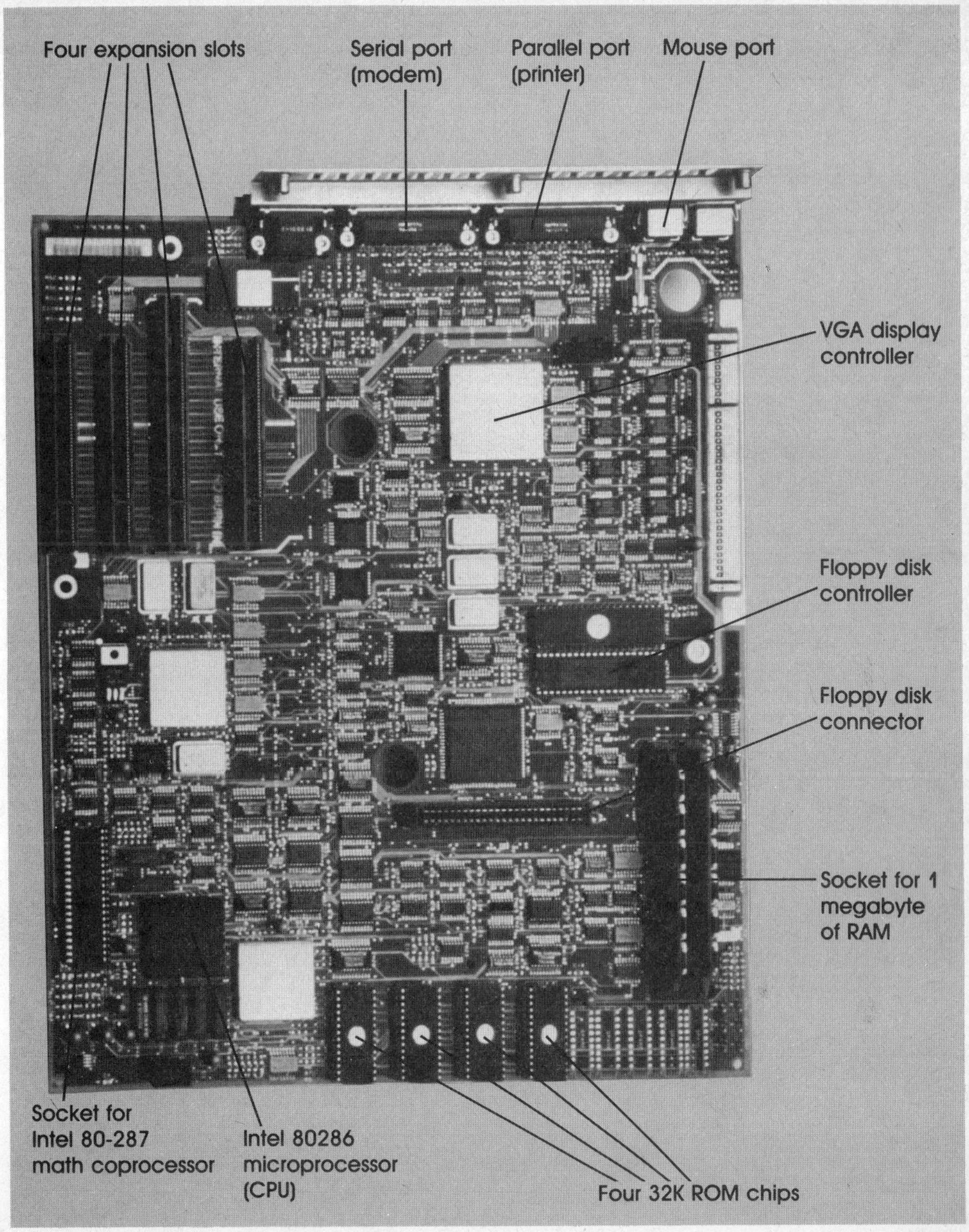

Microprocessor

As we said, the microprocessor is a microcomputer's central processing unit (CPU). It consists of a single integrated circuit chip that is usually soldered or plugged into a socket on the motherboard (see Figure 1.4). IBM and IBM-compatible microcomputers use microprocessors from the Intel 8088 family, which includes the 8088, 8086, 80286, and 80386 chips. The 8088 is used in older IBM and IBM-compatibles such as the original IBM Personal Computer and PC/XT. The slightly more efficient 8086 chip is used in IBM's newer low-end models, such as the IBM Personal System/2 Models 25 and 30. The more powerful 80286 chip is used in mid-range microcomputers, such as the original IBM Personal Computer AT and the newer IBM Personal System/2 Models 50 and 60. Finally, the very powerful and fast 80386 chip is used in high-end models, such as the IBM Personal System/2 Models 70 and 80.

Memory

Memory is a computer's internal storage, used to hold programs and data. Also called **primary storage**, memory is measured in bytes. A **byte** is the amount of storage needed to hold a single character, such as the letter A. Since computers can store many thousands or millions of bytes, the terms **kilobyte (K)** and **megabyte (M)** are often used. One kilobyte or 1K is equal to 1024 bytes. One megabyte or 1M is equal to 1,048,576 bytes. In general, microcomputer memory is made up of two types of integrated circuit chips: RAM and ROM.

RAM, which stands for **Random Access Memory**, is temporary storage. Programs and data can be stored there while they are being used and then overwritten by other programs and data later. When the computer is turned off, RAM loses its contents. Most microcomputers can now have at least 640K of RAM on their motherboards. Many can have much more installed on expansion boards. For example, the IBM Personal System/2 Model 80 can be equipped with up to 16 megabytes of RAM.

ROM, which stands for **Read Only Memory**, is permanent storage. The contents of ROM chips, which are encoded at the factory, remain intact when the computer is turned off. The programs and data permanently stored in ROM can be read and used, but never erased, changed, or augmented. Many microcomputers use ROM to store programs and data that are used frequently but need never be changed, such as portions of the operating system. Most microcomputers contain at least one ROM chip as part of their primary storage. The IBM Personal System/2 Model 50, for example, uses four 32K ROM chips on the motherboard to store essential programs and data (see Figure 1.4).

Disk Drives

A **disk drive** is a piece of equipment that can read and write programs and data on magnetic disks. A **magnetic disk** is a semi-permanent storage medium that can be erased and rewritten many times. Most microcomputers can now be equipped with two basic kinds of disk drives: floppy disk drives and hard disk drives.

A **floppy disk drive** works with **floppy disks** (also called **diskettes**), which are inexpensive, flexible magnetic disks encased in plastic (see Figure 1.5). Floppy disks can be inserted and removed from their disk drives. The IBM Personal System/2 Model 50, for example, accepts a 3½-inch diskette, which can hold up to 1.44 megabytes of programs and data. Although most newer microcomputers now come with 3½-inch disk drives, many microcomputers still use 5¼-inch floppy disk

Figure 1.5 Floppy Disks

drives. A typical 5¼-inch floppy disk holds 360K, but there are some drives that use 5¼-inch disks that hold 1.2 megabytes.

A **hard disk drive** uses one or more magnetic metal platters to hold programs and data (see Figure 1.6). Most hard disk drives have their magnetic disks permanently sealed inside. These disks are rigid, much faster, and have much greater capacity than floppy disks. Hard disk drives come in sizes ranging from 10 megabytes to several hundred megabytes. The most popular sizes are now 20, 30, and 40 megabytes. The IBM Personal System/2 Model 50, for example, comes standard with a 20 megabyte internal hard disk. On a microcomputer with a hard disk, programs are usually run from the hard disk. The floppy disk drive is generally relegated to copying software to or from the hard disk and making backup copies of important programs and data.

Figure 1.6 Hard Disk Drive

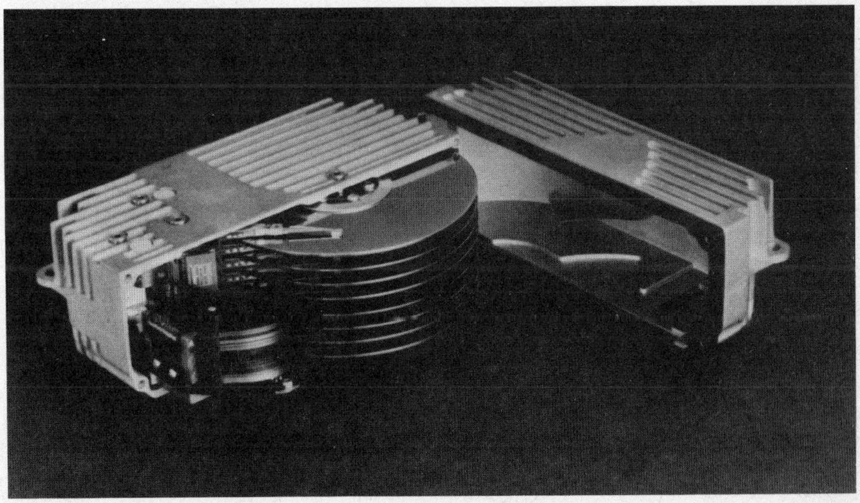

Display

A display, also called a **monitor**, is similar in many ways to an ordinary television screen. The display is used to present text and **graphics**, which are simply any kind of pictures, drawings, charts, or plots. The vast majority of computer monitors create text and graphics on the screen with tiny dots called **pixels** (short for picture elements). The number and size of these pixels determine a monitor's sharpness or **resolution**. There are three basic types of displays:

- **Monochrome Text** These monitors can only display letters, numbers, punctuation, and a limited set of other symbols in just one color, usually green on black, amber on black, white on black, or black on white.
- **Monochrome Graphics** In addition to text, these monitors can also display graphics on the screen. Only one color can be presented, but different shades of that color may be used.
- **Color Graphics** These monitors can display text and graphics in more than one color.

The capabilities of a particular display system are dependent on both the monitor itself and its device controller. The device controller for the display system is called a **display adapter**. For IBM and IBM-compatible microcomputers, there are several different display adapters that can be used. Some of these follow.

- **Monochrome Display Adapter (MDA)** This is the controller used with early low-end IBM microcomputers. It can only display text on a monochrome screen, but it generates very crisp, easy to read characters.
- **Color Graphics Adapter (CGA)** This is IBM's first microcomputer color graphics adapter. It can do color graphics, but the quality is rather poor. In other words, its low resolution makes text and graphics look rather fuzzy. Furthermore, the CGA is limited to a maximum of only 16 different colors, of which only only four can be on the screen at the same time.
- **Hercules Graphics Adapter** This adapter, made by Hercules Computer Technology, acts as a monochrome display adapter, but adds monochrome graphics capability.
- **Enhanced Graphics Adapter (EGA)** This color graphics adapter from IBM can do everything the CGA can do, yet is much better than the CGA. The resolution is significantly higher and the maximum number of different colors on the screen is 16 out of 64 possible choices.
- **Multi-Color Graphics Array (MCGA)** This is the display adapter built onto the motherboards of the IBM Personal System/2 Models 25 and 30. It can be used with either a monochrome graphics or color graphics monitor. It's maximum resolution is better than the EGA and can display a maximum of 256 different colors on the screen at once out of 262,144 possible choices.
- **Video Graphics Array (VGA)** This is the display adapter built onto the motherboards of the IBM Personal System/2 Models 50, 60, 70, and 80. It can also be purchased as a separate expansion board for other types of IBM and IBM-compatible computers. Slightly more advanced than the MCGA, the VGA can also do everything the EGA can do.

Keyboard

The keyboard is the primary device for entering text and telling the computer what to do. It is similar, in many respects, to a typewriter keyboard. Many microcomputers also have an auxiliary input device known as a **mouse**. This little box, which is glided across the table top, allows the user to manipulate objects on the display screen and select actions to be performed by pressing one or more buttons.

For IBM and IBM-compatible microcomputers, there are three basic keyboard designs. These are the original IBM Personal Computer keyboard, the original IBM Personal Computer AT keyboard, and the new IBM Enhanced Keyboard. Figure 1.7 shows all three of these keyboards. Besides the usual letters and punctuation marks that you're likely to find on any typewriter, a computer keyboard has other important keys:

- **Enter (or Return)** Analogous to the carriage return on a typewriter, this key is used to signal the end of an entry. Basically, it tells the computer to go ahead and process what was just typed.
- **Backspace** Like the Backspace key on a typewriter, this key is used to go back and type over a previously typed character.
- **Shift** Located at either side of the keyboard, one of the Shift keys is held down while pressing another key to produce a capital letter or the symbol shown on the top part of the key.
- **Caps Lock** This key is like the Caps Lock key on a typewriter, except that it works for only letter keys. When the caps lock key is pressed, capital letters will appear when you press letter keys. When Caps Lock is pressed again, small letters will appear when their keys are pressed.
- **Tab** Like the Tab key on a typewriter, this key is used to advance to the next tab stop.

Figure 1.7 (top) Original IBM PC Keyboard, (center) "AT-Style" Keyboard, and (bottom) IBM Enhanced Keyboard

- **Escape** The Escape key (abbreviated **Esc**) is often used to cancel a previously typed entry or to prematurely end a program.
- **Break** This key is very much like the Escape key and is used by some programs in a similar fashion.
- **Control** Somewhat like a Shift key, the Control key (abbreviated **Ctrl**) is pressed in conjunction with other keys. It's used to control a program's actions by sending certain codes to the computer.
- **Alternate** Very similar to the Control key, the Alternate key (abbreviated **Alt**) is also pressed in conjunction with other keys. It's used to give an alternate meaning to the keys pressed along with it.
- **Insert** This key (abbreviated **Ins**) is often used to insert a new entry between existing entries.

- **Delete** This key (abbreviated **Del**) is often used to erase an entry or a single character.
- **Function Keys** These are keys that are pressed to activate frequently used operations within a program. They are used differently by different programs. IBM-compatible keyboards have either 10 function keys along the left side or 12 function keys across the top. The function keys are labeled with an F followed by a number, like this: F1, F2, F3, etc.
- **Cursor Movement Keys** Most programs use these keys to let you move the **cursor** (a little blinking underscore or box) around the screen. In a word processing program, for example, the cursor marks the place where text is inserted, deleted, or otherwise manipulated. The cursor movement keys include Up Arrow, Down Arrow, Left Arrow, Right Arrow, Home, End, Page Up, and Page Down.
- **Numeric Keypad** This is an array of keys at the right side of a keyboard that resembles the layout of a calculator's keys. It includes the ten digits and other symbols that facilitate the entry of numbers and formulas. On the IBM PC and AT keyboards, the numeric keypad is superimposed on the cursor movement keys.
- **Num Lock** This key is used to switch the function of the numeric keypad. In one state, the numeric keypad acts as number keys. In the other state, the numeric keypad acts as cursor movement keys. You press the Num Lock key to switch between these two states.
- **Print Screen** If you have a printer, this key is pressed to send a copy of the current screen to your printer. On some keyboards, it is abbreviated **PrtSc**.
- **Pause** This key is used to temporarily suspend the operation of the current program.
- **Scroll Lock** This key is not used by very many programs and it has no standard function. Some programs use it to switch the Cursor Movement keys into a state in which they can move (or scroll) the whole screen up, down, left, or right.

Printer

A **printer** is a device used to produce permanent copies of text and possibly graphics on paper. Although a printer is not absolutely necessary to run most programs, it is an extremely useful addition to a microcomputer system. This is because computers are commonly used to produce letters, reports, books, tables, figures, charts, graphs, diagrams, maps, and pictures. Paper output, or *hard copy* as it's also called, is a convenient medium for distributing and communicating this work to others. The four kinds of printers most frequently used with microcomputers are dot-matrix printers, daisy-wheel printers, ink-jet printers, and laser printers.

Dot-Matrix Printers

A **dot-matrix printer** is an output device that uses tiny dots to create text and graphics on paper (see Figure 1.8). Just as graphics monitors use pixels to construct characters and pictures on a screen, dot-matrix printers similarly use dots of ink on pages of paper. Inside the dot-matrix printer a *printhead* is moved across the paper from left to right, and sometimes also from right to left (see Figure 1.8). This printhead may contain anywhere from 7 to 27 pins arranged in a vertical column. While most dot-matrix printers use 9 pins, more expensive printers with 18 or 24 pins are also fairly common. As the printhead moves horizontally, it

Figure 1.8 (a) The Printhead of a Dot-Matrix Printer, (b) The Process of Printing a Dot-Matrix Character, (c) The pattern of dots within the matrix that form the character, and (d) An IBM Proprinter XL24, a dot-matrix printer

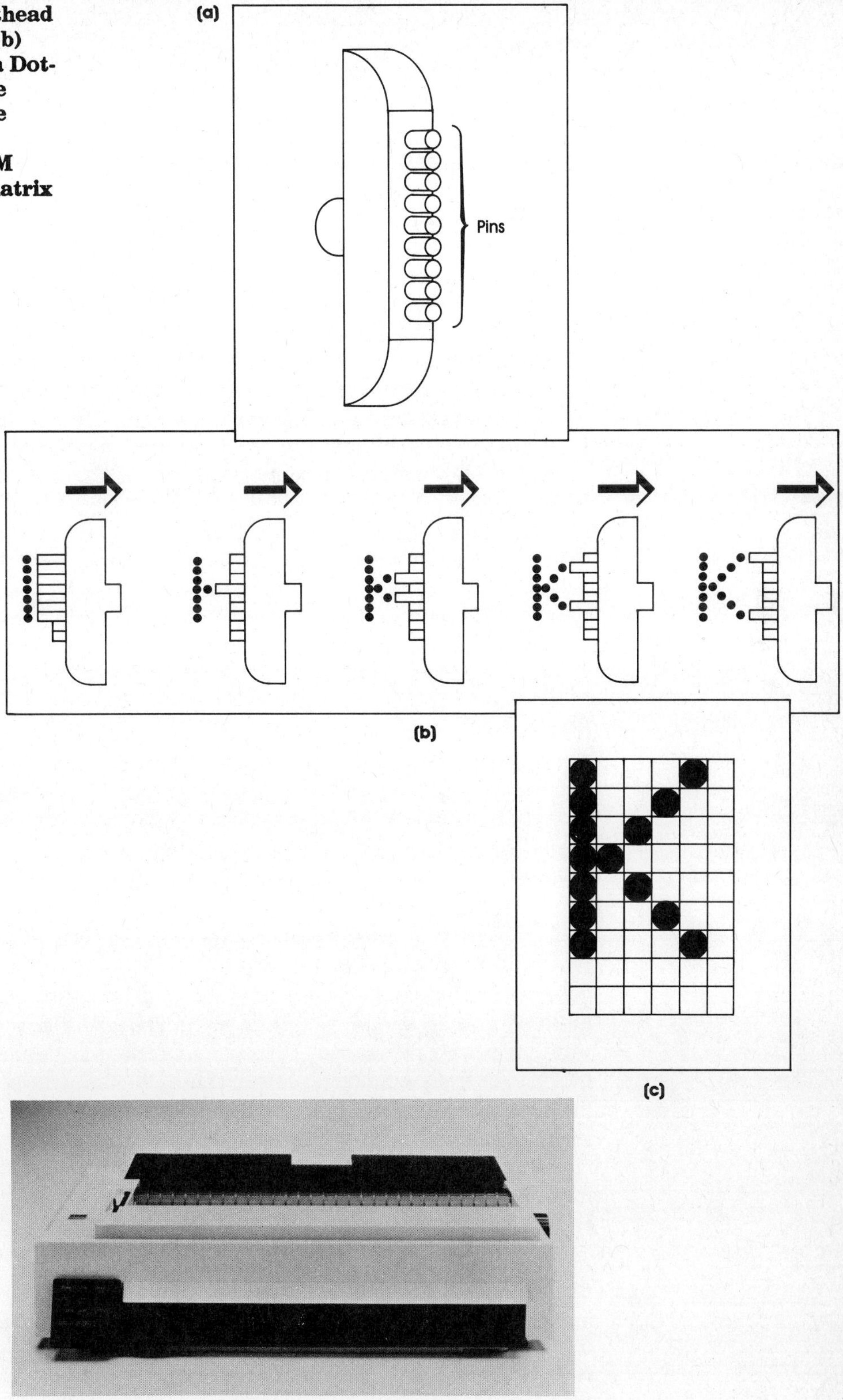

constructs a character by repeatedly striking these pins against an inked ribbon and the paper. Electrical signals cause the appropriate pins to be thrust out at the proper moment to form the successive columns of dots that make up a character's image. Each column of the character is struck in turn against the ribbon and paper until the complete image has been formed. Dot-matrix printers are sometimes described as being impact printers because of the way the pins hit the ribbon and paper. This printing mechanism is most frequently used for text, but dot-matrix printers can usually produce graphics, too.

Dot-matrix printers are by far the most popular type of microcomputer printer. They are reasonably priced, fairly quick, and pretty reliable. Prices range between $150 and $3000, but the typical cost of an average 9-pin dot-matrix printer is about $500. The speed of a dot-matrix printer depends upon what print mode it is using. The fastest mode is called **draft mode**, in which characters are formed by just a single pass of the print head. Some expensive dot-matrix printers are able to achieve speeds of 400 characters per second in draft mode. Many dot-matrix printers also have a **near letter-quality (NLQ) mode**. In this mode, the printhead makes two or more passes over each character, slightly shifting its position each time. This tends to fill in the gaps between the dots and makes text appear more like it was produced by an electric typewriter. Using NLQ mode may slow some printers down to only 15 characters per second. Generating graphics with a dot-matrix printer can also be time consuming. Depending upon how dark the images are, it may take several minutes per page to produce graphics on a dot-matrix printer.

Daisy-Wheel Printers

A **daisy-wheel printer** uses a circular printing mechanism called a **daisy wheel**. Solid, raised characters are embossed on the ends of little "arms" arranged in a circle like the spokes of a wheel or the petals of a daisy. As this daisy wheel spins, a tiny, stationary hammer strikes the back of the proper character when it passes (see Figure 1.9). This impact drives the character pattern, which is embossed in reverse, against an inked ribbon and the paper. Daisy-wheel printers are true **letter-quality** printers because they produce well-defined text just like electric typewriters. Their prices are comparable with that of dot-matrix printers. Unlike dot-matrix printers, however, daisy-wheel printers cannot produce graphics. They are also noisier and slower than dot-matrix printers. The typical daisy-wheel printer can only print about 10 characters per second, and even the most expensive models generally cannot do better than 100 characters per second. Daisy-wheel printers are still fairly popular with microcomputer owners, but they are gradually being supplanted by 24-pin dot-matrix printers and laser printers.

Ink-Jet Printers

An **ink-jet printer** has a mechanism that squirts tiny, electrically-charged droplets of ink out of a nozzle and onto the paper (see Figure 1.10). (No pins or hammers strike the paper, so ink-jet printers are classified as nonimpact printers.) Ink-jet printers are fast, quiet, and can produce high-quality print, but they are slightly more expensive than dot-matrix printers. Some ink-jet printers have a tendency to clog their nozzle with ink and smear characters on paper. Many ink-jet printers, however, have the capability to print in color, a capability most other types of printers lack.

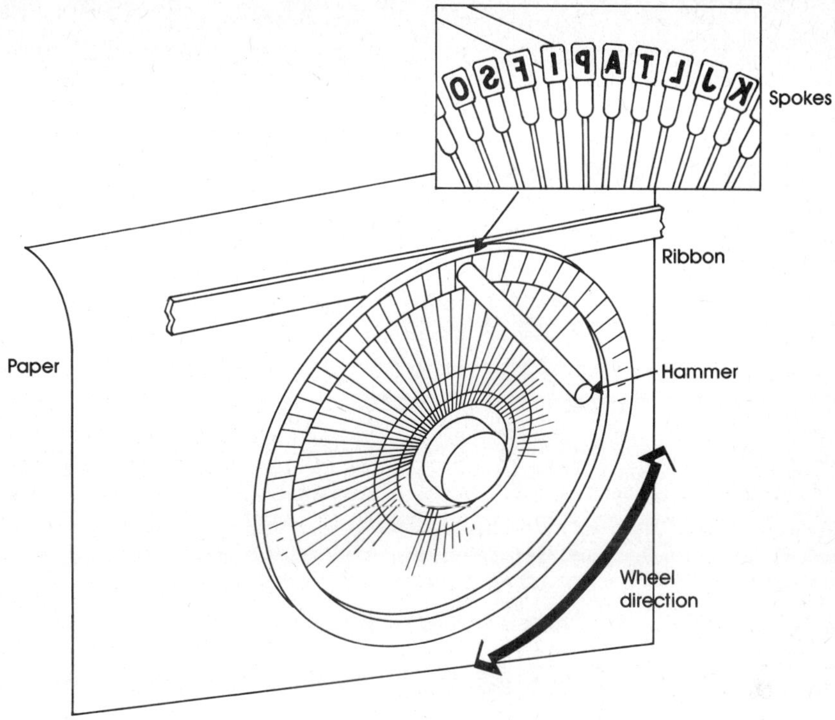

Figure 1.9 The Daisy-Wheel Printing Mechanism and a Daisy Wheel

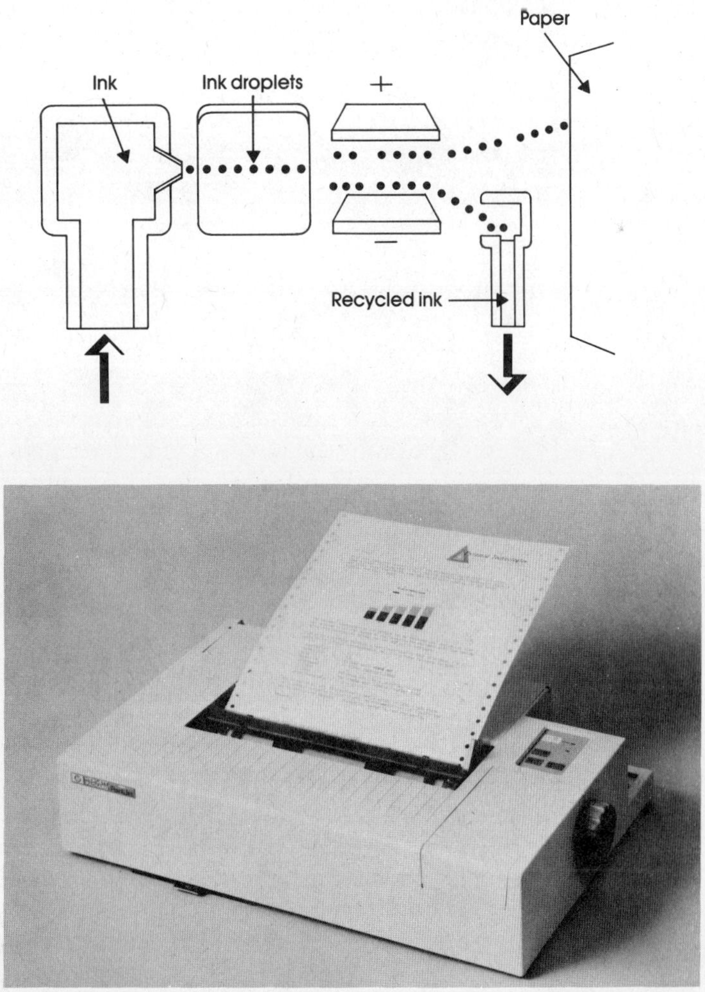

Figure 1.10 (above) Ink Jet Printing, and (below) The Hewlett-Packard PaintJet Color-Graphics Printer

Laser Printers

A **laser printer** is an output device that uses tightly focused beams of light to transfer images to paper (see Figure 1.11). A tiny laser emits pulsating pinpoint bursts of light that are reflected off a special spinning mirror. This mirror reflects light onto a rotating drum. Light striking the drum causes it to become charged with electricity. An inklike toner is attracted to the drum in these electrically charged spots. When the drum is rolled over a piece of paper, the toner is transferred to the paper and an image is permanently fixed through a combination of heat and pressure. This image transfer process is similar to that found in a plain-paper photocopy machine. The result is high-quality text and graphics that almost look as if they were typeset. (Like ink-jet printers, laser printers are classified as nonimpact printers.)

Laser printers represent the most advanced printing technology. Although the images they produce are made up of dots, these dots are much smaller and more densely packed than the dots created with a dot-matrix printer. The typical microcomputer laser printer is capable of printing at a resolution of 300 dots per inch, both horizontally and vertically. This means 90,000 dots per square inch. Besides printing high-quality images, laser printers are also fast and quiet. The average speed of most laser printers is 8 pages per minute. This is equivalent to about 400 characters per second. Because laser printers don't use impact methods like dot-matrix and daisy-wheel printers, they are very quiet by comparison. The major disadvantage to laser printers is their cost. Prices generally start at around $1000. Despite the cost, more and more laser printers are being used with microcomputers every year. They are especially popular in office situations where the printer can be shared among several users.

Figure 1.11 The Hewlett-Packard LaserJet Series II Laser Printer

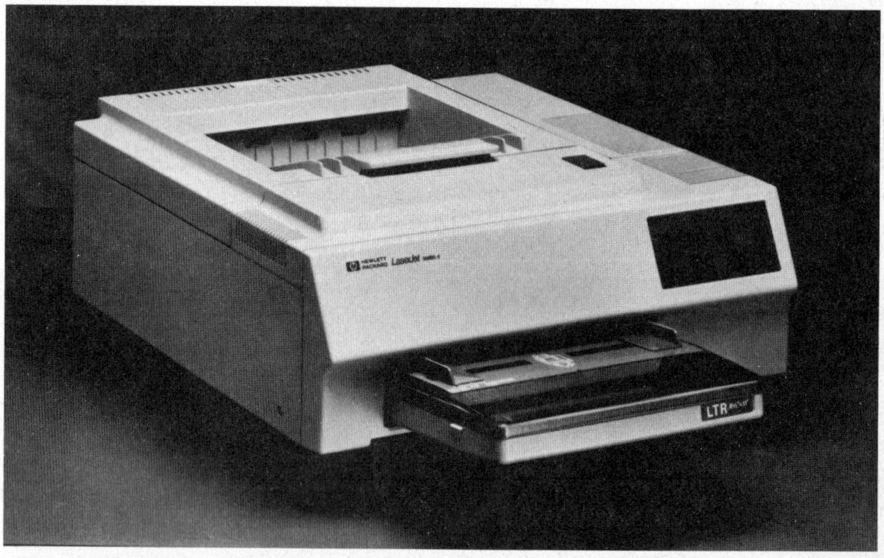

Software

By itself, computer hardware is useless. Programs are needed to operate the hardware. As we mentioned earlier, a program is simply a sequence of instructions that tells a computer what to do. **Software** is a general term that refers to any single program or group of programs. In contrast to hardware, which is constructed from physical materials like metal and plastic, software is built from knowledge, planning, and testing. A person who creates programs is called a **programmer**. Programmers use their knowledge of how a computer works to plan sets of instructions that accomplish useful tasks. These instructions are entered into the computer and repeatedly tested and modified until they achieve the desired results. As we said earlier, programs and data are generally kept on magnetic disks, where they can be accessed and used over and over again. Note that the disks themselves aren't the software, they're just the medium on which software is stored.

As an analogy, think of a stereo system. The amplifier, compact disc player, and speakers are the hardware. The amplifier is like the central processing unit and memory, the compact disc player is like a disk drive, and the speakers are like the display, except they present audio instead of video output. The music, which is stored on compact discs, is like software, which is stored on floppy disks. Just as you can amass a huge music collection by buying more compact discs, you can build a bigger software library by purchasing additional programs on floppy disks. The stereo system is of little use without the compact discs and the compact discs are useless without the stereo system. Similarly, a computer system is useless without software and software is useless without a computer system on which to run it.

Just as there are different types of hardware, there are also different types of software. Basically, there are three major categories: *system software*, *programming languages*, and *application software*.

System Software

System software handles the many details of managing a computer system. A computer's **operating system** makes up most of its system software. This is the set of programs that controls a computer's hardware and manages the use of software. One small part of the operating system, for example, is a program that identifies which key you've pressed, determines the character that corresponds to that key, and forms that character on the display screen. Another example is a program that lets you erase the contents of a magnetic disk. Some system software is built into a computer's ROM chips, while other system software comes on magnetic disk and must be purchased separately.

Programming Languages

Computer programs are developed with programming languages. A **programming language** is simply a set of symbols and rules to direct the operations of a computer. There are many different programming languages in common use, each designed to develop certain types of programs. A few of the most popular programming languages are BASIC, Pascal, C, FORTRAN, COBOL, and Ada. Although it can be helpful to learn a programming language for some very specific applications, most people who use computers don't actually program them. They just use programs, such as operating systems and application software, that have been developed by professional programmers.

Application Software

Application software is the software that applies the computer to useful tasks such as helping you create documents, figure your taxes, maintain mailing lists, and draw charts. Also called **application packages** or simply **applications**, these programs are the real reason most people buy and use microcomputers. The three most widely used applications follow.

- **Word Processing** A **word processing package** is software that helps you prepare documents by letting you enter, store, modify, format, copy, and print text.
- **Spreadsheet** A **spreadsheet package** is software that lets you manipulate tables of numbers, text, and formulas. It is an extremely flexible tool that can be used to handle typical accounting chores, monitor investments, balance a checkbook, and work out a budget.
- **Data Base Management** A **data base** is an organized collection of one or more files of related data. A file is a mass of individual data items kept together on a disk. A **data base management package** is software that lets you create, add to, delete from, update, rearrange, select from, print out, and otherwise administer data files such as mailing lists and inventories.

Besides these "big three" application packages, there are many other types of popular software, including the following:

- **Communications** Using an auxiliary device called a **modem**, a computer can transmit and receive programs and data over ordinary telephone lines. Communications software makes it possible for a computer to use a modem to call other computers and access on-line information services.
- **Graphics** Graphics packages let you use a computer to create all kinds of pictures including graphs, charts, maps, paintings, drawings, diagrams, blueprints, simulated slide shows, and animated presentations.
- **Desktop Publishing** Combining the results of word processing and graphics, desktop publishing or page layout software lets you use a computer and laser printer to produce near typeset quality documents.
- **Accounting** Accounting software lets you use a computer to record, analyze, and report business transactions.
- **Integrated Software** Integrated software combines word processing, spreadsheet, data base management, communications, and graphics applications in a single package.
- **Windowing Environment** Working closely with the operating system, a windowing environment allows you to divide your screen into a number of different boxes, or *windows*, and run a separate program in each one.
- **DOS Shell** A DOS shell is a program that enhances PC-DOS or MS-DOS, the operating system used with IBM and IBM-compatible microcomputers. Basically, it is an easy-to-use front-end to DOS that helps you execute commands and manage disk files.
- **Utilities** There are a host of small, specific programs called utilities that add handy features and functions to a particular operating system or application package. These include disk and file utilities, printer utilities, keyboard utilities, and desk accessories such as calculators, calendars, and address books.
- **On-Line References** Software to help you check your spelling, find a synonym, or look up a word's definition are all examples of on-line references.
- **Statistics and Math** Many programs exist for performing statistical analyses and helping solve mathematical equations.
- **Project Management** A project management package is software that helps you formally plan and control complex undertakings, such as the construction of a building, the development of a new product, or the installation of a large computer system.
- **Personal Finance and Taxes** Many programs exist for helping you manage your money and prepare your federal and state income tax returns.
- **Education** There is a wide range of programs for teaching skills and concepts, from learning the alphabet to designing physics experiments.

- **Entertainment** An amazing variety of microcomputer software exists for playing games, simulating cars and planes, and playing music.
- **Hypertext** A hypertext package is software that lets you store and retrieve all kinds of information in a nonsequential manner. In other words, you can randomly jump from topic to related topic, accessing any kind of information the computer can store, including text, graphics, audio, and video.
- **Expert System** An expert system is a computer program that contains a collection of facts and a list of rules for making inferences about those facts. Such software can use these facts and rules in a particular field to advise, analyze, categorize, diagnose, explain, identify, interpret, and teach.

Helpful Hints for Using a Microcomputer

Now that we've covered the general topics, let's go over a few specific details that can help prepare you for using a microcomputer.

Turning on the Computer

Sometimes, just turning on the computer can be an adventure. It seems that some manufacturers are fond of "hiding" the **power switch**. This has the practical purpose of making it difficult to turn off the computer by accident while in the middle of some critical task. Not being able to find the power switch, however, can make you feel lost before you even begin.

On the new IBM Personal System/2 computers, the power switch is a big red toggle right up front on the system unit. No problem here. On other computers, if the switch isn't immediately obvious up front, then it is probably on the right side of the system unit toward the rear. This is the case in IBM PCs, XTs, and ATs. Some models from other companies have the power switch mounted somewhere on the back side of the system unit or monitor.

Speaking of monitors, many color graphics displays have a separate power switch that must also be turned on, otherwise you will be looking at a permanently blank screen. The on/off switch is usually the top knob of three on the front of the monitor and is turned on by rotating it to the right. The other two knobs are the contrast and brightness controls, just like the ones on many television sets. If these three controls aren't right up front, they may be present as slightly protruding little disks located just under the bottom front edge of the monitor. Another possibility is the ever-popular back side of the monitor.

Operating the Printer

Like the system unit and monitor, the printer also has a power switch that must be turned on. This power switch is frequently positioned at the rear of the left or right side. In addition, there are at least three other buttons on most printers. Usually stationed on the top or front of the printer, these three buttons may be labeled On Line, Line Feed, and Form Feed. The **On Line** button is very important and is usually paired with an indicator light. When the On Line light is on, the printer is connected to and controlled by the computer, so that printing can occur. Make sure the On Line button is pressed so that the On Line light is on before attempting to print. The **Line Feed** and **Form Feed** buttons let you advance the paper in the printer, usually only when the printer is off line.

Caring for Floppy Disks

Although floppy disks are quite durable and can take quite a bit of punishment, there are a few guidelines you should follow in their handling:

1. Don't touch the exposed surfaces on 5¼-inch disks. Don't open the little metal door on 3½-inch disks.
2. Don't bend or fold 5¼-inch floppies.
3. Don't expose disks to extreme heat.
4. Keep 5¼-inch disks in their sleeves when not in use.
5. Don't write on 5¼-inch disks with pencils or hard point pens.
6. Keep your disks dry.
7. Don't expose disks to strong magnetic fields (keep them away from magnets and powerful motors).
8. Always try to keep at least one backup copy of all important disks.
9. Carefully insert and remove disks from disk drives. Wait until the drive's red access light is off before changing disks.

Conclusion

In this chapter of the *Software Guide*, you've learned what a microcomputer is, what it does, and what kinds of software are available. In addition, you've learned a few tips for turning on a microcomputer, operating a printer, and caring for floppy disks. This material sets the stage for the next chapter, in which you will complete lessons to teach you how to use PC-DOS and MS-DOS, the operating systems for IBM and IBM-compatible microcomputers.

Exercises

Multiple Choice

Choose the best selection to complete each statement.

____________ 1. A microcomputer is a computer in which the central processing unit consists of
 (a) a RAM chip. (c) a microprocessor chip.
 (b) a ROM chip. (d) a device controller chip.

____________ 2. A set of instructions that controls a computer's operation is
 (a) a program. (c) input.
 (b) data. (d) output.

____________ 3. The main circuit board of a computer is called the
 (a) expansion board. (c) bus.
 (b) device controller. (d) motherboard or system board.

____________ 4. IBM and IBM-compatible microcomputers use microprocessors from the
 (a) Motorola 68000 family. (c) Zilog Z80 family.
 (b) Intel 8088 family. (d) GTE G65SC816 family.

____________ 5. A byte is the amount of storage needed to hold a
 (a) single character. (c) single line.
 (b) single page. (d) single file.

__________ 6. Which of the following does NOT describe random access memory (RAM)?
(a) It is temporary storage.
(b) It loses its contents when the power is turned off.
(c) It is permanently encoded at the factory.
(d) It can be read and written over and over again.

__________ 7. The two most popular floppy disk sizes are
(a) 3½-inch and 8-inch.
(b) 5¼-inch and 8-inch.
(c) 3½-inch and 5¼-inch.
(d) 3-inch and 12-inch.

__________ 8. Which of the following types of display systems can present text and pictures on the screen, but in only a single color?
(a) monochrome text display
(b) monochrome graphics display
(c) color graphics display
(d) monochrome display adapter

__________ 9. Which of the following microcomputer keyboard keys is used to tell the computer to go ahead and process what was just typed?
(a) Enter or Return key
(b) Escape key
(c) Control key
(d) Function key

__________ 10. The most advanced and expensive type of printer in the following group is the
(a) dot-matrix printer.
(b) daisy-wheel printer.
(c) ink-jet printer.
(d) laser printer.

__________ 11. A set of programs that controls a computer's hardware and manages the use of software is called
(a) an operating system.
(b) a programming language.
(c) an application package.
(d) a data base management package.

__________ 12. Which of the following types of software lets you manipulate tables of numbers, text, and formulas?
(a) word processing package
(b) spreadsheet package
(c) data base management package
(d) operating system

__________ 13. Which of the following types of software lets you use a modem to transmit and receive programs and data over ordinary telephone lines?
(a) communications package
(b) graphics package
(c) desktop publishing package
(d) windowing package

__________ 14. Which of the following types of software lets you use a computer to record, analyze, and report business transactions?
(a) graphics package
(b) accounting package
(c) DOS shell
(d) utilities

__________ 15. Small, specific programs that add handy features and functions to a particular operating system or application package are called
(a) on-line references.
(b) hypertext programs.
(c) spreadsheets.
(d) utilities.

__________ 16. Which of the following types of software would be the best choice for maintaining a mailing list?
(a) word processing package
(b) spreadsheet package
(c) data base management package
(d) accounting package

__________ 17. Which of the following types of programs would you use to help plan and control the construction of a new office building?
(a) word processing package
(b) spreadsheet package
(c) integrated software package
(d) project management package

_____ 18. Which of the following types of software lets you store and retrieve all kinds of information in a nonsequential manner and then randomly jump from topic to related topic?
(a) word processing package
(b) spreadsheet package
(c) hypertext package
(d) expert system

_____ 19. Which printer button determines whether the printer is connected to and controlled by the computer?
(a) Power
(b) On Line
(c) Line Feed
(d) Form Feed

_____ 20. Which of the following should you NOT do to a floppy disk?
(a) Keep it in its sleeve when not in use.
(b) Keep it away from extreme heat.
(c) Keep it near a magnet when not in use.
(d) Keep it dry.

Fill-In

1. An __________ microcomputer works like a comparable IBM model and can run the same software.

2. At the lowest level, the basic operations of all computers can be summed up as input, __________, and output.

3. The __________ of a computer system is the electronic and mechanical equipment that make it work.

4. A microcomputer's motherboard contains the __________, which is a set of wires and connectors that link the CPU to memory and other computer components.

5. __________ is temporary storage for programs and data, which can be used and then overwritten by other programs and data. __________, on the other hand, is permanent storage encoded at the factory with frequently used programs and data that need never be changed.

6. Most microcomputers can be equipped with two basic types of disk drives: floppy disk drives and __________.

7. The number and size of a monitor's __________ determine its sharpness, or resolution.

8. The __________ is the display adapter that comes built onto the motherboards of high-end IBM Personal System/2 microcomputers.

9. Many microcomputers have an auxiliary input device known as a __________, which is a little box with one or more buttons that is glided across the table top.

10. On an IBM keyboard, the __________ Movement keys include Up Arrow, Down Arrow, Left Arrow, Right Arrow, Home, End, Page Up and Page Down.

11. __________ printers are by far the most popular type of microcomputer printer.

12. __________ is a general term that refers to any single program or group of programs.

13. BASIC, Pascal, C, FORTRAN, COBOL, and Ada are all examples of popular programming __________.

14. ___________________ software is the software that applies the computer to useful tasks such as helping you create documents, prepare a budget, or maintain a mailing list.

15. ___________________ packages let you use a computer to create all kinds of graphs, charts, maps, paintings, drawings, diagrams, slide shows, and presentations.

16. Combining the results of word processing and graphics software, ___________________ software lets you use a computer and laser printer to produce near typeset quality documents.

17. ___________________ software combines word processing, spreadsheet, data base management, communications, and graphics applications in a single package.

18. A ___________________ environment allows you to divide your screen into a number of different boxes and run a separate program in each one.

19. A ___________________ management package is software that helps you formally plan and control complex undertakings.

20. An ___________________ system is a computer program that contains a collection of facts and a list of rules for making inferences about those facts.

2

The PC-DOS Operating System

Learning Objectives

After reading this chapter, you should know how to do the following:

- Explain what a disk operating system is
- Explain why there are different versions of PC-DOS
- Boot PC-DOS with the computer turned off
- Boot PC-DOS with the computer turned on
- Obtain a directory listing of a disk's files
- Explain the structure of a PC-DOS file name
- Use the special PC-DOS keys
- Change the default disk drive
- Obtain a disk and memory status report
- Clear the display screen
- Format a diskette
- Format a system diskette
- Copy files
- Copy entire diskettes
- Change file names
- Erase files
- Display a text file on the screen
- Send a text file to the printer
- Run an application program
- Create and use DOS subdirectories
- Use DOS batch files

Introduction

An operating system is a set of programs that helps you use the hardware and software resources of a general-purpose computer. It's what you use to tell the computer to perform common tasks such as running application packages, managing disk storage, and controlling peripheral devices such as display screens and printers. In one sense, an operating system is like a toolbox that contains all kinds of utility programs to perform many of the little jobs that most users need. These utilities are like tools; some are used everyday by almost everyone, while others are more exotic and may only be used occasionally, even by experts.

A **disk operating system** (or **DOS**) is kept on a floppy or hard disk. When the computer system is turned on, some components of the operating system are loaded from disk into primary memory and remain there until the computer is shut off. These components, called **resident routines** or **internal commands**, are kept in memory because they are the most essential or the most frequently used parts of the operating system. The other components of a DOS are kept on disk and are temporarily loaded into memory only when they are needed or specifically requested. As a result, these latter commands are often called **transient routines** or **external commands**.

An important characteristic of a disk operating system is the abundance of utilities to deal with files that are stored on disks. A file, you'll recall, is just a collection of related data that is kept on a disk. Since most programs, text, and numerical data are kept in disk files, almost everything you do with computers involves working with files. Every computer user, therefore, must deal with an operating system to some extent. This chapter of the guide will teach you how to use the most popular disk operating system for IBM and IBM-compatible microcomputers.

PC-DOS and MS-DOS

PC-DOS, which stands for *Personal Computer Disk Operating System*, is by far the most popular operating system IBM offers for its microcomputers. It was written for IBM by Microsoft Corporation, which kept the right to also sell the same operating system itself under its own name, **MS-DOS**. Although there are some minor differences between PC-DOS and MS-DOS, from the average user's viewpoint they are virtually identical. The major distinction is that PC-DOS is generally used with IBM computers, and MS-DOS is used with the many compatible computers made by companies such as Compaq, AT&T, Tandy, and Zenith. From now on, everything we say about PC-DOS will also be true for MS-DOS, and so we'll just refer to both of them generically as DOS.

DOS Versions

Because computer technology changes so rapidly, an operating system like DOS is not a static entity. Operating systems must be constantly updated to accommodate new computer models and new capabilities for existing models. So far, there have been several official releases, or versions, of DOS. Although bugs have been worked out and improvements made over previous versions, the driving force behind each new release of DOS has been a new hardware capability, usually related to floppy or hard disk drives.

It's important to know which version of DOS you are using, because some hardware and software can only be used with more recent versions. Fortunately, each new version of DOS is **upwardly compatible** with former versions–that is, almost everything that worked with previous versions should work with the new version. So, you probably don't have to change the way you did things before unless you want to take advantage of the added capabilities of the new version. In fact, you usually don't have to buy the latest version of DOS each time a new release is issued. As long as the version you have works with your hardware and software, you can continue using it.

DOS versions are denoted by numbers such as 1.00, 2.10, and 3.30. The number to the left of the decimal point reflects a major classification; the numbers to the right represent more minor differences. The bigger the number, the more recent the version. Table 2.1 shows a summary of the DOS versions that have been released so far. Throughout this guide, we'll be using DOS 3.30 for all of our examples. Don't be concerned if you don't have the same version of DOS; everything we'll be covering will work for all versions 2.00 or newer.

Table 2.1

Version	Date	Hardware Support (Reason for New Version)
1.00	8/81	IBM PC single-sided floppy disk drive
1.10	5/82	IBM PC double-sided floppy disk drive
2.00	3/83	IBM XT 10 megabyte hard disk drive
2.10	10/83	IBM PCjr & Portable PC half-height floppy
3.00	8/84	IBM AT high-capacity floppy & hard disk
3.10	3/85	IBM AT network disks
3.20	12/85	IBM PC Convertible 3½-inch disk drive
3.30	3/87	IBM Personal System/2 disk drives
4.00	7/88	Hard disks larger than 35 megabytes

General Features of PC-DOS

PC-DOS provides many capabilities, both simple and complex. We'll be discussing some of its most used simple features, such as the following:

- **Booting Up with the Power Off** DOS can automatically load itself into memory when you turn the power on.
- **Booting Up with the Power On** DOS can be reloaded and reset without having to turn the power off and then on again.
- **Keeping Track of the Date and Time** Once you initially tell DOS the date and time, it will keep track of them until you turn the computer off or reboot.
- **Listing File Directories** You can instruct DOS to produce a directory of some or all of the files on a particular disk.
- **Using Special Keys** By pressing certain keys on the keyboard, you can tell DOS to cancel an input line, pause screen scrolling, cancel a command, print the screen, and echo input and output to the printer.
- **Changing the Default Drive** DOS lets you specify the disk drive it will assume when a drive designation isn't explicitly given.
- **Checking Disk and Memory Status** DOS can produce a report of useful information about a disk and primary memory.
- **Clearing the Screen** DOS lets you erase your display screen.
- **Formatting a Diskette** DOS lets you prepare a new diskette so that program and data files can be stored on it. It can also install itself on a new diskette if you tell it to do so.
- **Copying Files** DOS permits you to copy files onto the same disk or from one disk to another.
- **Copying Diskettes** DOS allows you to copy an entire diskette with a single command.
- **Changing File Names** DOS lets you choose new names for existing files.
- **Erasing Files** DOS allows you to delete unneeded files from a disk.
- **Displaying Text Files** You can have DOS display text files on your screen.
- **Printing Text Files** You can have DOS send text files to your printer.
- **Running Programs** You can tell DOS to run application programs such as VP-Planner Plus.
- **Using Subdirectories** You can create, use, and remove subdirectories, which are like separate little disks on a large disk.
- **Using Batch Files** You can create and execute collections of DOS commands stored in special text files called batch files.

Getting Started

Although DOS is a rich and powerful microcomputer operating system, you can quite easily learn its most commonly used features. For the most part, these features are invoked by issuing commands to DOS. A **command** is simply a word or mnemonic (memory aid) abbreviation entered at the keyboard that tells DOS to run a particular program. Once DOS has been initially loaded into memory, it's constantly on the lookout for these commands. In the following lessons you'll learn most of the DOS commands you're likely to need. You'll also be introduced to general concepts about the keyboard, display, disks, and disk drives that you'll be using in this and later parts. Wherever it's useful, figures will actually show you what you should see on your computer screen at a given point. These screen views will help you as you go through each lesson's steps.

DOS 3.30 comes on two floppy disks; one is labeled DOS Startup and the other is entitled DOS Operating. Previous versions of DOS also came on two disks, but these were labeled DOS and DOS Supplemental Programs. If you are using one of these earlier versions of DOS, you just need the DOS disk. If you are using a computer with a hard disk or one connected to a local area network, DOS may already be installed on it, but you can still use the DOS floppy disk or disks for the following lessons.

As you go through the lessons, you will be given instructions on what to type. In this text we'll use **bold** print to indicate what you're supposed to type. It doesn't matter whether you use uppercase or lowercase. DOS ignores case when processing commands.

Lesson 1: Booting DOS

The first thing that you must do is turn on your computer and load DOS into primary memory. This process is often called *booting DOS*, *loading DOS*, or simply *starting DOS*.

Step 1: Insert the DOS Disk

With the computer shut off, grasp the DOS 3.30 Startup disk (or DOS disk for previous versions) by the label and remove it from the sleeve (be careful not to touch the exposed parts around the oval slot and circular hole if it is a 5¼-inch disk). Hold the disk with the label side up and the oval slot pointing toward the computer. If your computer uses 3½-inch disks, hold the disk with the label up and the metal door pointed toward the computer. Insert the disk into the A drive and close the disk drive door. If your computer has two disk drives, side by side, the A drive is the one on the left. If it has two half-height drives arranged vertically, the A drive is the one on the top. If there is only one floppy drive, then it is the A drive.

Step 2: Turn the Computer On

If you have a color display, turn it on by twisting the top knob on the front panel to the right. If you have a monochrome display, you don't need to turn it on because its power cord is plugged into the computer. Turn on the computer by flipping up the big red switch, which is located right up front on the system unit of IBM Personal System/2 computers, or at the rear of the right side of the system unit on older IBM models. You should hear the cooling fan begin to whir.

Step 3: Watch the Display and Wait

Once the power is turned on, the computer goes through some self-tests to ensure that it is working properly. One of these tests checks out all of the primary memory installed. This could take a few seconds or several minutes depending upon how much memory the computer has. So, if nothing appears to be happening for a couple of minutes, don't be alarmed. After the power-on self-tests are complete, the computer will access drive A to see if the DOS disk is there. You should see the little red access light go on and hear the disk drive whir and click. Assuming the computer is in working order, the disk drive door is properly closed, and there is nothing wrong with the DOS disk, the DOS command processor and internal commands will be loaded into main memory and a message such as the following will appear on your display screen:

```
Current date is Tue  1-01-1980
Enter new date (mm-dd-yy): _
```

Step 4: Enter the Date and Time

Type today's date in the form of mm-dd-yy or mm/dd/yy. In other words, type in the month number, a dash or slash, the day of the month, another dash or slash, and the last two digits of the year. Now press the **Enter** key. After you have entered the date, a message like this will appear:

```
Current time is  0:00:36.90
Enter new time: _
```

Type the hour, a colon, and the minute, then press the **Enter** key. If it's afternoon, add twelve to the hour as in the military fashion. For example, if it's 2 P.M., enter **14:00**. You can enter the second and the hundreds of seconds if you happen to carry a stopwatch and feel so inclined. However, just the hour and minute are sufficient. After you do this, your screen should look something like the screen in Figure 2.1. The A> on the last line is called the **DOS prompt**. It indicates that disk drive A is your default drive and that the DOS command processor is patiently waiting for you to enter a command. The **default drive** is the disk drive that DOS assumes you want to use unless you specify otherwise.

Note: Many computers now have a battery-maintained clock/calendar that makes entering the date and time unnecessary. If the current date and time presented by DOS are correct, all you have to do is press the Enter key each time in response.

Figure 2.1 Booting Up DOS

```
Current date is Wed  1-01-1980
Enter new date (mm-dd-yy): 7-13-89
Current time is  0:00:36.26
Enter new time: 7:51


The IBM Personal Computer DOS
Version 3.30 (C)Copyright International Business Machines Corp 1981, 1987
             (C)Copyright Microsoft Corp 1981, 1986

A>_
```

Lesson 2: Rebooting DOS

Occasionally, something goes wrong in a program and the computer may seem to be "stuck." Or, after working with a program you may have to "reinitialize" the computer, or bring it back to the way it was when you first turned it on. You could, of course, just shut the computer off and boot it up as we outlined in Lesson 1. There's another way, however, to reboot the computer without shutting it off.

Step 1: Press Ctrl-Alt-Del

DOS has a special combination of keypresses that will reboot the computer without having to shut it off first. All you have to do is press the keys marked **Ctrl**, **Alt**, and **Del**, and hold them down at the same time for a moment.

Step 2: Watch the Display and Wait

In most cases, the screen will go blank, the computer will beep, and the disk drive will spin and blink its red access light just like it did when you first turned it on. If all this doesn't happen, a serious program error has probably overwritten a crucial part of DOS in memory and you will have to shut the computer off and boot it up as you did in Lesson 1. If all is well, DOS will again ask you to supply the date and time.

Step 3: Enter the Date and Time

After you enter the date and time as you did in Lesson 1, DOS will once again display its copyright message and the system prompt, as shown in Figure 2.1.

Lesson 3: Listing a Disk File Directory

As we mentioned before, programs, data, and text are kept on disks in files. Every file has a name, size, creation date, and creation time associated with it. DOS can display this information for you if you use the directory command.

Step 1: Enter the Directory Command

At the DOS prompt, type in the letters **dir** and press the **Enter** key. As with all DOS commands, it doesn't matter if you use uppercase or lowercase letters. DIR is is the abbreviation for the DOS directory command that will list the directory of the default disk on your display screen. Remember that the default disk is the one in the disk drive that DOS assumes you are currently working on, and its letter is indicated by the DOS prompt. Right now, your default disk drive should be A, so the DIR command will list the file names, sizes, and creation dates and times for all the files on the floppy disk in drive A. Figure 2.2 shows what the screen looks like when it stops scrolling.

Figure 2.2 Listing a Directory

```
COMMAND  COM    25307   3-17-87  12:00p
ANSI     SYS     1678   3-17-87  12:00p
COUNTRY  SYS    11285   3-17-87  12:00p
DISPLAY  SYS    11290   3-17-87  12:00p
DRIVER   SYS     1196   3-17-87  12:00p
FASTOPEN EXE     3919   3-17-87  12:00p
FDISK    COM    48216   3-18-87  12:00p
FORMAT   COM    11616   3-18-87  12:00p
KEYB     COM     9056   3-17-87  12:00p
KEYBOARD SYS    19766   3-17-87  12:00p
MODE     COM    15487   3-17-87  12:00p
NLSFUNC  EXE     3060   3-17-87  12:00p
PRINTER  SYS    13590   3-17-87  12:00p
REPLACE  EXE    11775   3-17-87  12:00p
SELECT   COM     4163   3-17-87  12:00p
SYS      COM     4766   3-17-87  12:00p
VDISK    SYS     3455   3-17-87  12:00p
XCOPY    EXE    11247   3-17-87  12:00p
EGA      CPI    49065   3-18-87  12:00p
LCD      CPI    10752   3-17-87  12:00p
4201     CPI    17089   3-18-87  12:00p
5202     CPI      459   3-17-87  12:00p
        22 File(s)      9216 bytes free

A>_
```

This is the directory of the PC-DOS 3.30 DOS Startup floppy disk. (If you are using a different version of DOS, the directory will be somewhat different.) Listed are the names, sizes, and creation dates and times of all the files on the DOS Startup disk. Notice that each file's name has two parts: a **primary file name**, which can be up to eight characters long, and a three-letter **extension**. We'll have more to say about this file name format later in this lesson. The number to the immediate right of each file's name is its size in bytes. A byte, you'll recall, is the amount of storage needed to hold a single character. Finally, listed with each file is the date and time it was created or last changed. So, for example, the file FORMAT.COM is made up of 11,616 bytes and was created at 12:00 P.M. on March 18, 1987.

At the very bottom of the listing, DOS informs you that there are 22 files in the directory and 9,216 bytes of empty room left on the disk. As you can imagine, it's pretty important to be able to see what's on a disk and how much room is left. For this reason, DIR is one of most frequently used DOS commands.

Incidentally, most of the files that you see in this directory listing with an extension of COM or EXE are external commands or transient routines of DOS. These are programs that reside on the DOS disk until you specifically call them up. In contrast, the DIR command is an internal command or resident routine. It too is a component program of DOS, but because it's used so frequently it's loaded into memory when DOS is booted and it's kept there. This means that DIR is not stored by itself in a separate file on the DOS disk; once you've booted up, you don't need the DOS disk in drive A to use the directory command.

Step 2: Examine Another Disk's Directory

The DIR command can also be used to list the directory of a disk in a drive other than the current default drive. You can do this by specifying the disk drive designation after typing dir. For example, to list the directory of a disk in drive B, you could enter this command:

dir b:

The **b:** is the designation for the B disk drive. If you have a computer with two floppy drives, remove the DOS disk from drive A, insert it into drive B, close the door, and enter **dir b:**. You should see the same directory listing you saw in Step 1 of this lesson. After you're done looking at the directory of drive B, make sure to put the DOS disk back into drive A.

If your computer has a hard disk drive and no second floppy drive, try entering **dir c:**. You should see some kind of directory listing, though it will probably be different from the one in Figure 2.2. This difference exists because many additional files are most likely stored on your hard disk. Note that the hard disk is usually referred to as the C drive regardless of whether a B floppy drive is installed.

Step 3: Look For a Specific File

Frequently, you'd like to be able to check if a particular file is on a disk without having to look at the entire directory. The DIR command can do this for you if you give it the name of the file you're looking for. All you have to do is enter the name of the file after typing dir. Then DOS either lists an abbreviated directory with only that file in it or tells you the file is not there. For example, enter this command:

dir a:format.com

Figure 2.3 shows what you should see on your screen.

DOS File Names This is a good time to digress a bit and discuss DOS file names in more detail. First of all, notice that each file in the directory you listed has a unique name. No two files in the same directory can have the same name because DOS wouldn't be able to tell them apart. Two files on different disks, however, can have the same name. As we mentioned before, a file's full name can consist of

Figure 2.3 Looking for a Specific File

```
A>dir a:format.com

 Volume in drive A has no label
 Directory of  A:\

FORMAT   COM     11616   3-18-87  12:00p
        1 File(s)      9216 bytes free

A>_
```

two parts: a primary filename and an optional extension. The first part, or **file name** as IBM calls it, can be from one to eight characters long. It can include any of the characters you see on the keyboard except for the following, which are considered invalid in file names:

. " / \ [ ] : | < > + = ; ,

The second part, an optional short name, is called an **extension**. It is separated from the primary filename by a period and has from one to three characters in it. These characters also can be any of the keyboard characters except those invalid ones we just listed. If a file's name does have an extension, you must use both parts when telling DOS to do something with that file. Extensions are most often used to further classify files. For example, here are some of the more common file name extensions along with the types of files they usually designate:

.COM DOS external command files and other programs
.EXE Executable program files
.SYS DOS system configuration and device driver files
.BAT DOS batch files
.BAS BASIC language source code files
.PAS Pascal language source code files
.FOR FORTRAN language source code files
.ASM Assembly language source code files
.TXT Ordinary text files
.ASC ASCII files
.DOC Document files for some word processing programs
.WKS Lotus 1-2-3 Release 1A worksheet files
.WK1 Lotus 1-2-3 Release 2 and 2.01 worksheet files
.DBF dBASE III PLUS data base files

Finally, a file name can be prefaced with the designation of the disk drive that it's on. For example, A:FORMAT.COM is the specification for the file containing the FORMAT command on the DOS disk in drive A. Note that the colon must be used to separate the disk drive letter from the filename.

Step 4: Look for a Specific Group of Files

Not only can the DIR command find a single file on a disk, it can also be used to list a group of files if their names have some characters in common. This is possible through the use of the DOS global filename characters, * and ?. These characters can be included in a filename or extension to give you greater flexibility in designating DOS files. The * character can be used in a file specification to symbolize any character or group of characters. For example, *.SYS means "any file with an extension of SYS." The ? character is used to symbolize any single character. For example, MO?E.COM means "any file that has an extension of COM and a four-letter filename beginning with MO and ending with an E." Both global file name characters can be used together in the same specification, too. For example, ????.* means "any file with at most four characters in its first part." Try these examples yourself:

dir *.sys
dir mo?e.com
dir ????.*

Figure 2.4 shows what you should see on your screen after entering the command **dir *.sys.**

Figure 2.4 Looking for a Group of Files

```
A>dir *.sys

 Volume in drive A has no label
 Directory of  A:\

ANSI     SYS      1678   3-17-87  12:00p
COUNTRY  SYS     11285   3-17-87  12:00p
DISPLAY  SYS     11290   3-17-87  12:00p
DRIVER   SYS      1196   3-17-87  12:00p
KEYBOARD SYS     19766   3-17-87  12:00p
PRINTER  SYS     13590   3-17-87  12:00p
VDISK    SYS      3455   3-17-87  12:00p
        7 File(s)      9216 bytes free

A>_
```

Lesson 4: Using Special DOS Keys

Like most software, DOS assigns special meanings to certain keys and combinations of keypresses. You've already learned some of these. For example, you know that you must press the Enter key after typing in a command. This tells DOS to go ahead and process that command. The Backspace key can be used to correct typing errors on a line before the Enter key has been pressed. Finally, you learned in Lesson 2 that pressing the Control (Ctrl), Alternate (Alt), and Delete (Del) keys all at the same time will reboot DOS without having to shut off and then turn the power back on. Let's explore some of the other keys DOS uses.

Step 1: Press the Escape Key to Cancel a Line

As you've probably already discovered, it's pretty easy to make typing mistakes when using a keyboard. If the command you're typing is short, and you haven't pressed the Enter key yet, the easiest way to fix a mistake is to backspace over it and retype it. If the command is long, or if you really messed up, you can cancel the entire line you just typed and start all over again. To do this, just press the Escape (Esc) key. For example, type the following line at the DOS prompt (but don't press the Enter key):

This line is really messed up!

Let's say what you really meant to type in was **dir**, and you realized your mistake before you pressed the Enter key. Just press **Escape** to cancel this line. When you do this, DOS will display a / (slash) after the exclamation point to signal that this line has been canceled and it will skip down to the next line so you can start over again. Enter **dir** and you'll see the familiar DOS directory again.

Step 2: Press Ctrl-Num Lock to Pause Screen Scrolling

As you watch the DOS directory scroll by on the screen, notice that the first part of it disappears off the top. Sometimes, information scrolls by before you get a chance to read it all. It would be nice if you could temporarily stop the screen so that you wouldn't have to take speed reading lessons to use the computer. Fortunately, DOS can accomplish this pause for you if you hold down the Control key and press the Num Lock key. On the newer IBM Enhanced style keyboards, you have to press the Pause key instead of Ctrl-Num Lock. In either case, this action will immediately pause any screen that is scrolling by. To resume scrolling, just press any key (except a Shift, Lock, Ctrl, or Alt key). Enter **dir** and press **Ctrl-Num Lock** or the **Pause** key. Figure 2.5 shows what can happen. You can pause and resume scrolling as many times as you wish.

Figure 2.5 Pausing Screen Scrolling

```
A>dir

 Volume in drive A has no label
 Directory of  A:\

COMMAND  COM    25307   3-17-87  12:00p
ANSI     SYS     1678   3-17-87  12:00p
COUNTRY  SYS    11285   3-17-87  12:00p
DISPLAY  SYS    11290   3-17-87  12:00p
DRIVER   SYS     1196   3-17-87  12:00p
FASTOPEN EXE     3919   3-17-87  12:00p
FDISK    COM    48216   3-18-87  12:00p
FORMAT   COM    11616   3-18-87  12:00p
KEYB     COM     9056   3-17-87  12:00p
KEYBOARD SYS    19766   3-17-87  12:00p
MODE     COM    15487   3-17-87  12:00p
NLSFUNC  EXE     3060   3-17-87  12:00p
PRINTER  SYS    13590   3-17-87  12:00p
REPLACE  EXE    11775   3-17-87  12:00p
SELECT   COM     4163   3-17-87  12:00p
SYS      COM     4766   3-17-87  12:00p
VDI
```

Step 3: Press Ctrl-Break to Cancel a Command

Let's say that you've entered **dir** by mistake and you don't want to wait for the whole directory to scroll by on the screen. Or perhaps you've seen enough and you just want to stop it. You can cancel a DOS command by pressing the Control and Break keys at the same time. This action stops a command from finishing its job normally. In many cases, Ctrl-Break will also terminate programs other than just DOS commands.

Enter **dir** and press **Ctrl-Break** to terminate the directory command before it would normally finish. Figure 2.6 shows how this might appear on your screen. The ^C signifies a Ctrl-C character which has canceled the command.

On IBM PC and AT style keyboards, the Break key is right next to the Num Lock key and it's also labeled Scroll Lock. On the newer IBM Enhanced style keyboards, the Break key is the same as the Pause key. On all types of keyboards, you can also cancel a command by holding down the Control key and typing a C. Note that Ctrl-Break (or Ctrl-C) is different from the Escape key. Escape will cancel a

Figure 2.6 Canceling a Command

```
A>dir

 Volume in drive A has no label
 Directory of  A:\

COMMAND  COM    25307   3-17-87  12:00p
ANSI     SYS     1678   3-17-87  12:00p
COUNTRY  SYS    11285   3-17-87  12:00p
DISPLAY  SYS    11290   3-17-87  12:00p
DRIVER   SYS     1196   3-17-87  12:00p
FASTOPEN EXE     3919   3-17-87  12:00p
FDISK    COM    48216   3-18-87  12:00p
FORMAT   COM   ^C

A>_
```

line typed in at the DOS prompt before the Enter key has been pressed. Ctrl-Break cancels a command after the Enter key has been pressed and the command is already executing.

Step 4: Press Shift-PrtSc to Print the Screen

Frequently there's a sequence of commands or some information on the screen that you'd like to save. If you have a printer connected to your computer, DOS can produce a hard copy of everything that's currently on the display screen. On IBM PC and AT style keyboards, you press one of the shift keys along with the key marked PrtSc (Print Screen). On the newer IBM Enhanced style keyboards, you simply press the key labeled Print Screen. If you don't have a printer, you'll just have to take our word for it; if you have a printer, make sure it's turned on and press **Shift-PrtSc** or press the **Print Screen** key. You should get a copy of what's on your screen right now.

Step 5: Press Ctrl-PrtSc to Echo to the Printer

Notice that the printout you got from the previous step contains only one screen of text. This output would be less than desirable if you wanted a hard copy of the entire DOS directory because the whole directory doesn't fit on a single screen at once. Pressing Ctrl-PrtSc (or Ctrl-Print Screen on the Enhanced style keyboards), however, will cause whatever you type and the computer's responses to be displayed both on the screen and sent to the printer. This echoing will continue until you press Ctrl-PrtSc again. So, you could, for example, get a hard copy of your entire computer session.

To get a hard copy of the DOS disk directory, press **Ctrl-PrtSc** and then enter **dir**. You should see the directory information being displayed on the screen a bit slower as it is also being sent to the printer. When it's done and you get the DOS prompt again, press **Ctrl-PrtSc** to turn off printer echoing.

Lesson 5: Changing the Default Disk Drive

So far, you've been doing all your work on the A disk drive. The DOS prompt has been A>, which indicates that drive A is your current default disk drive. Thus, whenever you enter a command that doesn't explicitly specify a particular disk drive, the A drive is assumed. For example, when you enter **dir**, you get a directory of the disk in the default drive, which is currently drive A. If your computer has more than one disk drive, and most IBMs and IBM-compatibles do, you may sometime want to change your default drive from A to B, or to C if you have a hard disk. DOS makes it easy to take advantage of this feature, which is also called *switching drives*.

Step 1: Enter the Designation of the New Default Drive

If you have a computer with two floppy drives, you can change your default drive from A to B by typing **b:** and pressing the **Enter** key. If you have a computer with a hard disk, you can change your default drive from A to the hard disk by typing **c:** and pressing the **Enter** key. As soon as you do this, DOS responds with a new prompt, which indicates the new default drive. So, if you have two floppy drives and you enter **b:**, DOS responds with B> as the new prompt. If you have a hard disk and you enter **c:**, DOS responds with C> as the new prompt.

Step 2: Use the New Default Drive

If you have two floppy drives, remove the DOS disk from drive A and put it into the B drive and close the door. Now enter a DIR command, such as **dir *.sys.** The directory listing you get now will be of the new default drive, B or C (see Figure 2.7). Although this might not seem terribly exciting at the moment, being able to change the default drive easily enables you to make full use of all of your installed disk drives. As you become more proficient with DOS and application packages, you'll find yourself switching default disk drives often. For example, on systems with two floppy drives, you may leave the DOS disk in drive A and a disk containing a particular application program in drive B. Then, after booting up, you would switch to drive B to run your application program.

Figure 2.7 Changing the Default Disk Drive

```
A>b:

B>dir *.sys

 Volume in drive B has no label
 Directory of  B:\

ANSI     SYS     1678   3-17-87  12:00p
COUNTRY  SYS    11285   3-17-87  12:00p
DISPLAY  SYS    11290   3-17-87  12:00p
DRIVER   SYS     1196   3-17-87  12:00p
KEYBOARD SYS    19766   3-17-87  12:00p
PRINTER  SYS    13590   3-17-87  12:00p
VDISK    SYS     3455   3-17-87  12:00p
        7 File(s)      9216 bytes free

B>a:

A>_
```

Step 3: Switch Back to Disk Drive A

Enter **a:** to change the default directory back to the A drive. If you put the DOS disk in drive B, remove it and put it back into the A drive.

Lesson 6: Checking Disk and Memory Status

You've already learned how to use the DIR command to examine the contents of a disk's directory. In addition to this, DOS provides a command that can display a status report about a disk and the memory installed in your computer. This report contains some interesting and useful information. With DOS 3.30, this command is on the DOS Operating disk. If you're using DOS 3.30, take the DOS Startup disk out of drive A and replace it with the DOS Operating disk. If you're using a previous version of DOS, you don't need to change disks.

Step 1: Enter CHKDSK

With the appropriate disk in drive A, type **chkdsk** and press the **Enter** key. This will invoke the DOS check disk command and produces a report on your screen that looks something like the Figure 2.8. If you're not using DOS version 3.30 or if your computer has more or less than 512 kilobytes (512K) of primary memory, the numbers in your report will be different.

Step 2: Examine the Status Report

This status report tells you several useful things. It tells you that the total capacity of the disk currently in the default drive is 362,496 bytes (equivalent to about 100 pages of text). Admittedly, the "0 bytes in 1 hidden files" statement doesn't make much sense. You can simply ignore it in this case. The hidden files mentioned in the report are parts of DOS that are kept on the disk, but do not appear in the disk

Figure 2.8 The CHKDSK Report

```
A>chkdsk

   362496 bytes total disk space
    53248 bytes in 3 hidden files
   300032 bytes in 22 user files
     9216 bytes available on disk

   524288 bytes total memory
   399984 bytes free

A>_
```

directory. These files contain important DOS programs that are kept hidden from you so that you don't rename, change, or delete them. The CHKDSK report then tells you that there are 31 ordinary user files on the disk and that they occupy 307,200 bytes of space. That leaves 55,296 bytes of empty space still on the disk. Finally, CHKDSK tells you that 524,288 bytes (or 512K) of primary memory are installed in this computer and that 472,064 bytes of these are free for use by application programs. The difference between these latter two figures, 52,224 bytes, is the amount of primary memory taken up by the parts of DOS that remain resident–the command processor and the internal commands.

Lesson 7: Clearing the Screen

By now, you've probably accumulated quite a collection of commands and directory listings on your screen. Although this does no harm, it can be a bit distracting. Or, perhaps you want to type a sequence of commands and then do a print screen, and you would like to start off with a clean slate. Don't worry, it's easy to tell DOS to erase the screen.

Step 1: Enter CLS

To clear the screen, simply type **cls** and press the **Enter** key. DOS will then erase everything from the screen and start you off again with the system prompt on the first line in the upper left corner.

Lesson 8: Formatting a Diskette

Before a new floppy disk can be used to store programs and data files, it must undergo an initial preparation known as formatting. This preparation is not done at the factory, so you must do it with your own computer for each brand new diskette you're going to use. Although you usually format a new diskette only once, you can format a previously formatted disk in order to clear it off completely. Formatting a floppy basically consists of the following procedures:

- Checking the diskette for bad spots
- Wiping out any information that might be on the diskette
- Building a directory that will hold information about the files that will be on the diskette
- Marking off the empty space into equal-sized chunks called **sectors**
- Copying DOS onto the diskette if specified to do so

The DOS FORMAT command can automatically do all this for you.

Step 1: Get a Floppy Disk to Format

For this lesson you'll need a new floppy disk or a previously used disk that can be completely erased. If you are going to format a diskette that's not new, double check to make sure it doesn't have any programs or data files on it that you want to keep. Formatting a disk erases everything that's on it.

If it is a used 5¼-inch diskette, also make sure that it doesn't have a write-protect tab on it. If you hold the diskette right side up with your thumb on the label, you should be able to see a little square notch cut into it on the left edge. If this notch is not covered up, then it's not write-protected and it's all right to use. If the diskette has a gummed tab covering the notch, then remove the tab. If the diskette has no notch, then it's permanently write-protected and you'll have to use another diskette.

Step 2: Put the DOS Startup Disk in A and the New Disk in B

On a computer with two floppy disk drives, make sure the DOS Startup disk is in drive A. Put the disk you want to format into drive B and close both doors. If your computer has only one floppy disk drive, just make sure the DOS Startup disk is in it. The FORMAT command will tell you when to put the new diskette in.

Step 3: Enter the FORMAT Command

On a computer with two floppy disk drives, type **format b:** and press the **Enter** key. On a computer with just one floppy drive, type **format a:** and press the **Enter** key. The FORMAT command will then tell you to insert the new diskette into drive B (for two-floppy systems) or drive A (for single-floppy systems). Insert the disk as indicated, and press the **Enter** key.

Step 4: Wait for FORMAT to Finish

The formatting procedure will take a minute or so, during which you should see the disk drive access light go on. When the procedure is done, the FORMAT command will tell you how much room is on the disk and if it contained any bad sectors. The command will then ask you if you want to format another diskette and you can enter **n** for no. You'll then get the DOS prompt back again. When you're done, your screen should look something Figure 2.9.

Figure 2.9 shows you that there are 362,496 bytes of total disk space and all of that space is available for files. In other words, no bad areas were detected. If there were any bad sectors found on the disk, less space would be available. DOS would mark these sectors as unusable and prevent them from being used to store files.

Figure 2.9 Formatting a Diskette

```
A>format b:
Insert new diskette for drive B:
and strike ENTER when ready

Format complete

    362496 bytes total disk space
    362496 bytes available on disk

Format another (Y/N)?n
A>_
```

Lesson 9: Formatting a System Diskette

The diskette you've just formatted can now be used to store programs and data files. It cannot, however, be used to boot the computer because it does not have DOS installed on it. If you want to format a diskette so that DOS is installed, the procedure is slightly different.

Step 1: Use the /S Parameter

Many DOS commands can be given options that specify a slightly different way of performing their tasks. The FORMAT command, for example, can be instructed to install the operating system on the disk it's preparing. To do this, simply type /s after the drive designator of the disk to format. The /s tells FORMAT to put the DOS internal commands and the command processor on the disk being formatted. You can try this out by reformatting the disk you just formatted as we outlined in Lesson 8. This time, however, enter this command:

format b:/s

Step 2: Examine the Disk's Directory

Now the FORMAT command will tell you that the system was transferred and that 78,848 bytes were used by the operating system. Only 283,648 bytes are left available on the disk. Enter **dir b:**. Your screen should look like Figure 2.10. Notice that only the file COMMAND.COM is on the new system disk. It does not contain any of the external command files that are on the DOS disk. So, although you could boot up with this new disk, and you could execute internal commands such as DIR, you could not use any external commands such as CHKDSK or FORMAT unless you somehow copied their command files onto it.

Figure 2.10 Formatting a System Diskette

```
A>format b:/s
Insert new diskette for drive B:
and strike ENTER when ready

Format complete
System transferred

    362496 bytes total disk space
     78848 bytes used by system
    283648 bytes available on disk

Format another (Y/N)?n
A>dir b:

 Volume in drive B has no label
 Directory of  B:\

COMMAND  COM    25307   3-17-87  12:00p
        1 File(s)    283648 bytes free

A>_
```

Lesson 10: Copying Files

Once a diskette has been formatted, it can be used to store program and data files. But how do you get files onto the new diskette? One way is by using the DOS COPY command. The COPY command can be used to duplicate one or more files on the same or on different diskettes. As a very versatile command, COPY can be used in several different ways.

Step 1: Copy a Single File (the Long Way)

Let's use the COPY command to copy a single file from the DOS Startup disk onto your newly formatted disk. For starters, we'll do it the longhand way and then we'll show you the shortcut. To copy the file FORMAT.COM from the DOS Startup disk onto your new disk, first make sure the DOS Startup disk is in drive A and the new disk is in drive B. Then enter this command:

copy a:format.com b:format.com

The first file name is the *source*, or what you're copying from–the file FORMAT.COM on the disk in drive A. The second file name is the *target*, or what you're copying to–a file named FORMAT.COM on the disk in drive B. After you do this, DOS will tell you that one file was copied. If you enter **dir b:** you should see the file FORMAT.COM in the directory of the disk in drive B. Figure 2.11 shows what you should see on your screen.

Figure 2.11 Copy a File

```
A>copy a:format.com b:format.com
        1 File(s) copied

A>dir b:

 Volume in drive B has no label
 Directory of  B:\

COMMAND  COM    25307   3-17-87  12:00p
FORMAT   COM    11616   3-18-87  12:00p
        2 File(s)    271360 bytes free

A>_
```

Step 2: Copy a Single File (the Short Way)

In most cases, if you omit certain information, DOS will assume the default values. For example, if you don't supply a disk drive designation in front of a filename, DOS will assume that you mean the default drive. Similarly, if you don't specify a name for the target file, the COPY command will assume that it is to use the same name as the source. This assumption will work as long as the source and the target files are on different disks. So, another way to copy FORMAT.COM would be to enter this command:

copy format.com b:

This command means copy the file FORMAT.COM on the disk in the default drive to the disk in drive B and give it the same name. Try this shorter command. Realize, however, that you will be copying the FORMAT.COM on drive A to the FORMAT.COM that already exists on drive B from our first copy operation. If you choose a name that already exists as the target, DOS will happily copy over it, destroying whatever was in that file before. Since we're copying the exact same file, there's no problem here. As a rule, however, you should be very careful about the name you choose for a target file. If it already exists on the disk you're copying to, the original version will be overwritten.

Step 3: Copy a Group of Files

By using the global file name characters * and ? we introduced in Lesson 3, you can copy several files all at once with a single COPY command. For example, with the DOS Startup disk in drive A and your newly formatted disk in drive B, enter this command:

copy *.* b:

This will copy every single file on the disk in the default drive to the disk in drive B. Figure 2.12 shows what your screen should look like when this command is completed.

Step 4: Copy a File to the Same Disk

All the examples we've covered so far have copied files from one disk to another. Also, the target file names have all been the same as the source file names. This arrangement, however, needn't always be so. The COPY command can be used to duplicate a file on the same disk. The only catch is that you have to choose a different name for the target. Remember that no two files in the same directory can have the same name.

Figure 2.12 Copying a Group of Files

```
COMMAND.COM
ANSI.SYS
COUNTRY.SYS
DISPLAY.SYS
DRIVER.SYS
FASTOPEN.EXE
FDISK.COM
FORMAT.COM
KEYB.COM
KEYBOARD.SYS
MODE.COM
NLSFUNC.EXE
PRINTER.SYS
REPLACE.EXE
SELECT.COM
SYS.COM
VDISK.SYS
XCOPY.EXE
EGA.CPI
LCD.CPI
4201.CPI
5202.CPI
        22 File(s) copied

A>_
```

One common reason for duplicating a file on the same disk with a different name is for backup purposes. Let's say that you are going to change an existing file. If that file is especially important, you might want to keep a copy of the original version before you change it. One of the great advantages of using computers is the ease with which they can copy files. So, before you change your file, make a copy of it and give the copy a different name. As an example, with your DOS disk in drive A and your newly formatted disk in drive B, enter this command:

copy b:format.com b:format.bak

This will create a copy of the FORMAT.COM file on the disk in drive B and it will be named FORMAT.BAK (BAK for backup). Now you can go ahead and make your modifications, safe in the knowledge that you've retained a copy of the original file.

Lesson 11: Copying an Entire Diskette

DOS has a more specific copy command that lets you copy an entire diskette all at once. What's more, this command automatically formats the target diskette if it's new. When you need an exact copy of an entire diskette, the DISKCOPY command can do the trick. DISKCOPY only works, however, if the source and target are the same type of disk. For instance, you cannot use the DISKCOPY command to duplicate the contents of a 5¼-inch diskette on a 3½-inch diskette. To see how the DISKCOPY command does work, let's make an exact copy of our DOS Startup diskette on the new diskette we've been working with.

Step 1: Put the DOS Operating Disk in Drive A

With DOS 3.30, DISKCOPY is an external command stored on the DOS Operating disk. So, the first step is to put the DOS Operating disk into drive A.

Step 2: Issue the DISKCOPY Command

If your computer has two identical floppy disk drives, enter this command:

diskcopy a: b:

If your computer has only one floppy drive or two drives that are of different types, such as a 5¼-inch drive and a 3½-inch drive, enter this command instead:

diskcopy a: a:

Step 3: Follow the Directions

The DISKCOPY command will tell you which drive to put your source and target diskettes into and when to do so. Remember: the DOS Startup diskette is the source, and the new diskette is the target. If your machine has only one floppy drive, you may have to swap the source and target diskettes in drive A several times. When it's done, DISKCOPY will ask you if you want to copy another diskette and you can enter **n** for no. If you have two floppy drives, Figure 2.13 shows what you should see on your screen when DISKCOPY is done.

Figure 2.13 Copying an Entire Diskette

```
A>diskcopy a: b:

Insert SOURCE diskette in drive A:

Insert TARGET diskette in drive B:

Press any key when ready . . .

Copying 40 tracks
9 Sectors/Track, 2 Side(s)


Copy another diskette (Y/N)?n


A>_
```

DISKCOPY is a very useful command for making backup copies of especially important diskettes. In fact, the documentation that comes with many software packages suggests that you use the DISKCOPY command to duplicate all of your original diskettes as soon as you get them. Furthermore, they say that you should put the originals away for safekeeping and only use your copies. Then, if you should accidentally erase something or if a diskette you use daily should become damaged or wear out, you would still have your original diskettes from which to make additional copies. These are good suggestions, and DISKCOPY will work fine as long as your software is not copy-protected.

Lesson 12: Changing File Names

When a file is originally created, the name it's given isn't set in stone; DOS lets you change file names very easily. Perhaps you've thought up a more appropriate name, or you want to abbreviate a long name. Another reason to change a file name is that you want to copy a file onto a disk that already has a file of the same name. If you don't change the name of the file already on the disk, copying a new file of the same name onto the disk will destroy the original file's contents. The DOS RENAME command allows you to change the names of one or more files.

Step 1: Rename a Single File

Changing a single file's name is quite easy. Just type rename (or its abbreviation, ren), followed by the file name you want to change, and then the new name that file is to have. For example, put the copy of the DOS Startup disk you made in Lesson 11 in drive A and enter this command:

rename format.com format.bak

Now enter this command to see what you've done:

dir format.*

Your screen should look like Figure 2.14. The directory shows that you've successfully changed the name of FORMAT.COM to FORMAT.BAK. This procedure would be very useful if you wanted to copy a new version of the FORMAT.COM file to your disk, yet still keep a copy of the original version. Since the backup version is safely stored as FORMAT.BAK, you could now copy a new FORMAT.COM onto your disk.

Figure 2.14 Renaming a File

```
A>rename format.com format.bak

A>dir format.*

 Volume in drive A has no label
 Directory of  A:\

FORMAT   BAK    11616   3-18-87  12:00p
        1 File(s)      9216 bytes free

A>_
```

Before you go on, change FORMAT.BAK back to FORMAT.COM so that the DOS Startup disk copy is like it was before. This time, however, try using the abbreviated form of the RENAME command:

ren format.bak format.com

Step 2: Rename Several Files at Once

By using the global file name characters * and ?, you can rename several files at once. For example, with a single command you could rename each file on your DOS Startup disk copy with an extension of EXE, and give it an extension of BAK. Try entering this command:

ren *.exe *.bak

Now enter this directory command to see what you've done:

dir *.bak

Your screen should look like Figure 2.15. There are now no files on your disk with EXE extensions. They all have BAK extensions instead. Before you go on, change them all back to the way they were with this command:

ren *.bak *.exe

Figure 2.15 Renaming a Group of Files

```
A>ren *.exe *.bak

A>dir *.bak

 Volume in drive A has no label
 Directory of  A:\

FASTOPEN BAK     3919   3-17-87  12:00p
NLSFUNC  BAK     3060   3-17-87  12:00p
REPLACE  BAK    11775   3-17-87  12:00p
XCOPY    BAK    11247   3-17-87  12:00p
        4 File(s)      9216 bytes free

A>_
```

Lesson 13: Erasing Files

Just as you accumulate old memos, notes, letters, and other scraps of this or that on your desk, disks can also become cluttered with unneeded files. Occasionally, it's necessary to clean up a bit and discard those items that you know you no longer need. Once you throw something away, however, it may be difficult or even impossible to get it back again. Be careful, therefore, to discard only files you're sure you can't use anymore. DOS makes it very easy to erase files, but it has no provision to unerase, or restore, them. Use the DOS ERASE command with caution.

Step 1: Erase a Single File

To erase a single file, just type in **erase** or **del** (for delete) and follow it with the name of the file you want to erase. Put your DOS Startup disk copy in drive A. Because it is a copy and you know that everything on it is also on the original DOS Startup disk, you can safely erase files. Nevertheless, we want to emphasize caution again. Data and programs are most frequently lost as the result of an accidentally or carelessly entered ERASE command than from any other cause. The original 5¼-inch disks that come with PC-DOS when you purchase it from IBM are permanently write-protected. They have no open square notches on the left edge. This means that you cannot delete any files from them with the ERASE command. The copy of the DOS disk you made in Lesson 11, however, is not write-protected, so you can erase files from it. Again make sure that your DOS Startup disk copy is in drive A, and enter this command to erase the FORMAT.COM file:

erase format.com

Now enter this directory command to see what you've done:

dir format.com

The file is now gone, so your screen should look like Figure 2.16.

Figure 2.16 Erasing a File

```
A>erase format.com

A>dir format.com

 Volume in drive A has no label
 Directory of  A:\

File not found

A>_
```

Step 2: Erasing Several Files All at Once

By using the global file name characters * and ?, you can tell DOS to erase several files with a single ERASE command. In fact, you can even wipe out every file on the whole disk. Although this is often useful to clear off a disk, it should be used with care. Make sure that your DOS Startup disk copy is in drive A, and enter this command:

erase *.*

Because this is a potentially disastrous command if entered by mistake, DOS will ask you if you're sure you want to do this. If you enter **y** for yes, DOS will go ahead and erase everything. If you say **n** for no, DOS will immediately cancel the ERASE command. You will only get this chance to back out, however, if you use the *.* designation. If you enter **erase *.exe**, DOS does not ask you if you're sure and immediately deletes all files with an extension of EXE. So again, *be careful* with the ERASE command!

Answer **y** to erase all the files and enter **dir** to examine the disk directory. Your screen should look like Figure 2.17.

Lesson 14: Displaying a Text File

So far, you've learned quite a bit about manipulating files with DOS. You haven't, however, yet looked inside one. The DOS TYPE command lets you display the contents of a file on the screen. Although TYPE will work with almost any file, unless it's a text file all you'll see is gibberish on the screen. A text file is one that is produced by a text editor or word processing program. Unfortunately, none of the files on the DOS disks are text files; they are all program files or system files. So, for the next two lessons we're going to use an interesting application of the COPY command to create a sample text file. Then we'll show you how to display that file on your screen and print it out.

Figure 2.17 Erasing All the Files

```
A>erase *.*
Are you sure (Y/N)?y

A>dir

 Volume in drive A has no label
 Directory of  A:\

File not found

A>_
```

Step 1: Create a Sample Text File

DOS has an interesting feature that lets you treat certain devices, such as the keyboard/screen combination or the printer, as if they were files. These devices are given reserved names that you can use as if they were file names. For example, the keyboard and screen together are given the reserved name CON, which stands for console. Similarly, the primary printer connected to the computer can be referred to as PRN. You can use these *device names* in DOS commands as if they were file names.

We're going to use this feature along with the COPY command to create a text file. Put the new diskette you first formatted in Lesson 8 into disk drive A and enter this command:

copy con readme.txt

This command tells DOS to take everything you now type at the keyboard and copy it into a new file named README.TXT. Type the following text, pressing the **Enter** key at the end of each line:

> This is a sample text file created to demonstrate the
> use of the DOS TYPE and PRINT commands. A text file is
> simply a file that contains only letters, numbers,
> punctuation marks, and other symbols that appear on the
> keyboard. Normally, text files are created with a text
> editor or word processing program. You can, however,
> create small text files directly from DOS by using the
> COPY command with the device name CON. When you are
> finished entering text, you must press the F6 function
> key and then the Enter key to generate an end-of-file
> code and have DOS copy the text file to your disk.

As the paragraph says, when you are finished entering the last line, press the **F6** function key and then press the **Enter** key. This inserts the DOS end-of-file code and completes the COPY command. Now enter **dir** to confirm that you have created the file on your disk. At this point, your screen should look like Figure 2.18.

Figure 2.18 Creating a Text File

```
A>copy con readme.txt
This is a sample text file created to demonstrate the
use of the DOS TYPE and PRINT commands.  A text file is
simply a file that contains only letters, numbers,
punctuation marks, and other symbols that appear on the
keyboard.  Normally, text files are created with a text
editor or word processing program.  You can, however,
create small text files directly from DOS by using the
COPY command with the device name CON.  When you are
finished entering text, you must press the F6 function
key and then the Enter key to generate an end-of-file
code and have DOS copy the text file to your disk.
^Z
        1 File(s) copied

A>dir

 Volume in drive A has no label
 Directory of  A:\

README   TXT       595   7-14-88  11:54a
        1 File(s)    308224 bytes free

A>_
```

Step 2: Issue the TYPE Command

There's now a file named README.TXT on your disk in drive A. You can see the contents of this file by using the DOS TYPE command. To use the TYPE command, simply enter **type** followed by the name of the file you wish to display. Enter this command to see what's in the file README.TXT:

type readme.txt

DOS will then display the contents of README.TXT on your screen, as shown in Figure 2.19.

Figure 2.19 Displaying a Text File

```
A>type readme.txt
This is a sample text file created to demonstrate the
use of the DOS TYPE and PRINT commands.  A text file is
simply a file that contains only letters, numbers,
punctuation marks, and other symbols that appear on the
keyboard.  Normally, text files are created with a text
editor or word processing program.  You can, however,
create small text files directly from DOS by using the
COPY command with the device name CON.  When you are
finished entering text, you must press the F6 function
key and then the Enter key to generate an end-of-file
code and have DOS copy the text file to your disk.

A>_
```

Lesson 15: Printing a Text File

Most text files eventually wind up on paper; after all, the end product of word processing is usually a hard copy document. The DOS PRINT command lets you send a text file directly to the printer, instead of displaying it on the screen. You'll need a printer for this lesson, as well as the diskette with the README.TXT file you created in Lesson 14.

Step 1: Put the DOS Operating Disk in Drive A

Unlike TYPE, the PRINT command is an external command that resides on the DOS Operating diskette. (DOS versions prior to 3.30 have the PRINT command on the diskette labeled DOS.) So, you must first put the disk containing the PRINT command into drive A. If your computer has two floppy drives, put the disk containing README.TXT in drive B.

Step 2: Turn on Your Printer

Before you can print a file, your printer must be turned on. Make sure that the power is on and that the printer is on-line, that is, connected to your computer.

Step 3: Issue the PRINT Command

To use the PRINT command, just type PRINT followed by the name of the file you want to print. You can preface the name of the file by the letter of the disk drive on which it is stored. Even if your computer has only one floppy drive, enter this command:

print b:readme.txt

After you do this, DOS will ask you to supply the following:

```
Name of list device [PRN]:
```

This rather cryptic request allows you to tell DOS which printer to use if you have more than one connected to your computer. The expression [PRN] means that unless you tell it otherwise, DOS will send the output to the default printer, which has the device name PRN. If you have only one printer, then it is the default printer. All you have to do here is just press the **Enter** key. DOS will ask you to supply the list device only the first time you use PRINT for any given computer session.

If you have a B floppy drive in your computer, PRINT will inform you that it's currently printing README.TXT and your printer should be merrily pounding away (unless, of course, it's a laser or ink-jet printer). Figure 2.20 shows what you should see on your screen.

If your computer only has one floppy drive, then DOS will ask you to do the following:

```
Insert diskette for drive B: and strike any key when ready.
```

Figure 2.20 Printing a Text File

```
A>print b:readme.txt
Name of list device [PRN]:
Resident part of PRINT installed

    B:\README.TXT is currently being printed

A>_
```

This is an example of a handy DOS feature. If you have only an A drive, and you issue a command that refers to drive B, DOS will temporarily pretend that drive A is drive B. It will then ask you to insert into drive A the disk you would have put into drive B if you had a drive B. So, if you have only one floppy drive, put the README.TXT disk in drive A when you get this message and press any key to finish the printing process.

The end result of this PRINT command will be a printout of the text in file README.TXT that you saw on your screen when you used the TYPE command in Lesson 14.

Lesson 16: Running a Program

This lesson won't really teach you anything new, because you've been running programs throughout this entire chapter. Every time you entered a DOS command, you were running a program. Remember: files with an EXE or COM extension are executable programs that you can run.

Step 1: Insert the Appropriate Disk

Just as you have to put the appropriate DOS disk in drive A when you want to use an external command, you must make sure a program is stored on a disk in one of your drives when you want to run the program. For example, to run an application program such as VP-Planner Plus, you must have its disk in the A or B drive. Or, if your computer has a hard disk, you could run the program off the C drive provided that a copy resides there. If your computer is connected to a local area network, you could run the program if it's stored on your network's server disk. DOS must be able to find a program before it can be run.

Step 2: Switch to the Appropriate Drive, if Necessary

For example, if you have two floppy drives, the DOS disk in A, and the application's program disk in B, you could switch to drive B as you learned in Lesson 5. The alternative to switching drives is to preface the program name you enter with the letter of the drive on which the program's file is stored.

Step 3: Type the Program Name and Press the Enter Key

As you now know, you invoke an external DOS command by entering its name along with any necessary file names and other information. In this sense, application programs such as VP-Planner Plus are the same as DOS external commands; all you have to do to run them is type the name of the EXE or COM file in which they're stored and press the **Enter** key. So, for example, to run the VP-Planner Plus program off your current default drive, just type **vpp** and press the **Enter** key. Or, if your default drive is A and the VP-Planner Plus disk is in drive B, you could enter **b:vpp** from the A drive to run the program. When you do either of these, DOS will load the VP-Planner Plus program into primary memory and begin executing it.

Lesson 17: Working with Subdirectories

As you can imagine, people who use microcomputers extensively often generate large numbers of files. Before hard disks became common, users had many different floppy disks on which to store their files. Organizing files meant physically organizing diskettes by keeping them well-labeled and storing them in subdivided boxes, racks, or cabinets. Once hard disks became common, however, operating systems had to devise a better method of organizing large numbers of files. Even a modest 20-megabyte hard disk can store thousands of different files. Looking for a particular file among hundreds or thousands of files is time consuming and tedious. Consequently, most microcomputer operating systems, including DOS, have evolved a **hierarchical** method of organizing files into groups. Such a system allows you to cluster files into orders or ranks, each subordinate to the one above. These groups of files, called **subdirectories**, are like file folders that can be nested within one another. Disks can be organized into subdirectories, each of which can contain files and other subdirectories.

Subdirectories are invaluable tools for organizing programs and data files on high-capacity storage devices. In addition, subdirectories make it easier for the operating system to locate a particular file because large numbers of files are divided into smaller groups. Although subdirectories are most often, indeed almost always, found on hard disks, they are occasionally used on floppy disks, too. DOS includes commands that let you create, access, and remove subdirectories.

With DOS, every disk has a single main directory, known as the **root directory**. DOS automatically creates a root directory on every disk you format. This is the directory you are in when you first boot up DOS or when you first change your default drive. The root directory itself has no name, but it's represented by a backslash (\).

Step 1: Create a Subdirectory

Let's create a subdirectory on the new floppy disk you have used in previous lessons (the one with README.TXT on it). Put this disk into drive A, and enter this command:

md a:\text

The internal DOS command MD or MKDIR (short for Make Directory) is used to create a new subdirectory. It is followed by the **path** of the new subdirectory. The path is an optional disk drive specifier followed by a list of subdirectory names, separated by backslashes. The rules for naming subdirectories are the same as the rules for naming files. The simplest path is a single backslash \, which represents the root directory of your current default drive. The command you just entered creates a subdirectory named TEXT on the disk in drive A. This subdirectory is one level below the root directory.

Step 2: Change to the Subdirectory

Think of the subdirectory as a separate "sub-disk" on your disk. Enter **dir** to display a directory of your disk. Now enter the Change Directory (CD or CHDIR) command to move into your new subdirectory:

cd a:\text

Enter **dir** again and Figure 2.21 shows what you should see on your screen. The first DIR gives a directory listing of the root directory of the floppy disk. It contains the README.TXT file and the TEXT subdirectory. The second DIR gives a directory listing inside the TEXT subdirectory.

Figure 2.21 Changing to a Subdirectory

```
A>md a:\text

A>dir

 Volume in drive A has no label
 Directory of  A:\

README   TXT      595   7-14-88  11:54a
TEXT         <DIR>      7-14-88   2:31p
        2 File(s)    307200 bytes free

A>cd a:\text

A>dir

 Volume in drive A has no label
 Directory of  A:\TEXT

.            <DIR>      7-14-88   2:31p
..           <DIR>      7-14-88   2:31p
        2 File(s)    307200 bytes free

A>_
```

Step 3: Copy a File to the Subdirectory

Right now, the TEXT subdirectory has no ordinary user files in it. You can, however, copy your own files to this subdirectory just as if it were a separate disk. For example, let's copy the README.TXT file from the root directory to the TEXT subdirectory. Enter this command:

copy a:\readme.txt

This command copies the file README.TXT from the root directory of drive A to your current subdirectory, which happens to be TEXT. Now enter **dir** and you'll see that a copy of README.TXT now also exists in the TEXT subdirectory. It's important to realize that there are two separate copies of README.TXT now on the disk: one in the root directory and one in the TEXT subdirectory.

Step 4: Remove the Subdirectory

Once you're in a subdirectory, you can almost think of it as a separate disk. You can run programs from within a subdirectory. Many DOS commands that deal with files will operate only on the files in your current subdirectory unless you specify otherwise. For example, you can delete every file in a subdirectory without affecting any files in the root directory or any other subdirectories. For example, try entering this command:

erase *.*

Answer **y** for yes when the ERASE command asks if you are sure that this is what you want to do. DOS will erase every file in your current directory, the TEXT subdirectory. Enter **dir** to see that this is true. Now change back to the root directory by entering this command:

cd a:

Now enter another DIR command and you will see that the README.TXT file in the root is still intact.

Just as you must occasionally delete unneeded files, sometimes subdirectories must be removed, too. Let's say that you are finished with the TEXT subdirectory and you want to remove it from your disk. To do this you must first erase any files inside the subdirectory and move out of the subdirectory. We've already done this. Now you can enter the Remove Directory command (RD or RMDIR) to remove the empty TEXT subdirectory from your disk:

rd a:\text

If you enter **dir**, you will see that the TEXT subdirectory has indeed been removed, and your disk is the same as it was when you began this lesson.

Lesson 18: Using Batch Files

A **batch file** is a text file that contains a list of commands or programs to be run. Batch files are usually created with a text editor or word processing program, but you can easily create short ones using the COPY command method we outlined in Step 1 of Lesson 14. In DOS, every batch file must have an extension of BAT. Once it has been created, a batch file is invoked by typing its filename and pressing the **Enter** key. When this is done, DOS executes each command or program listed in the batch file, one at a time. DOS includes features that enable experienced users to construct complex and very helpful batch files. Even if you never actually make your own batch files, you will undoubtedly use some made by others or included with application packages. As an example, let's create and use a simple batch file.

Step 1: Create the Batch File

As we said, batch files are usually created with a text editor or word processor. Short ones, however, can be easily created with the COPY command. At this point, you should still have the floppy disk with the README.TXT file on it in drive A. Enter this command to create a new batch file named SHOW.BAT on your current disk:

copy con show.bat

Now you can enter the text that will go inside the file SHOW.BAT. Type the following three commands, pressing the **Enter** key after each one:

cls
dir
type readme.txt

Finally, press the **F6** function key to generate the end-of-file code and then press the **Enter** key. Enter **dir** to examine the current contents of your disk and see that the batch file has indeed been created. Your screen should look like Figure 2.22.

Figure 2.22 Creating a Batch File

```
A>copy con show.bat
cls
dir
type readme.txt
^Z
        1 File(s) copied

A>dir

 Volume in drive A has no label
 Directory of  A:\

README   TXT      595   7-14-88  11:54a
SHOW     BAT       27   7-15-88   9:14a
        2 File(s)    307200 bytes free

A>_
```

Step 2: Use the Batch File

Running a batch file is just like executing a command or running an application program. You type its filename (without the extension) and press the Enter key. To run your newly created batch file, simply type **show** and press the **Enter** key. Figure 2.23 shows the result.

Figure 2.23 Using a Batch File

```
A>dir

 Volume in drive A has no label
 Directory of  A:\

README   TXT       595   7-14-88  11:54a
SHOW     BAT        27   7-15-88   9:14a
        2 File(s)    307200 bytes free

A>type readme.txt
This is a sample text file created to demonstrate the
use of the DOS TYPE and PRINT commands.  A text file is
simply a file that contains only letters, numbers,
punctuation marks, and other symbols that appear on the
keyboard.  Normally, text files are created with a text
editor or word processing program.  You can, however,
create small text files directly from DOS by using the
COPY command with the device name CON.  When you are
finished entering text, you must press the F6 function
key and then the Enter key to generate an end-of-file
code and have DOS copy the text file to your disk.

A>
A>_
```

Most commands and programs that you can run directly from the DOS prompt can be put inside a batch file. Batch files allow you to automate frequently executed series of commands. They also allow experts to set up complex sequences of commands to be run by novices. For example, many new application programs must be installed on your system before you can use them. In some cases, this installation process can be quite involved. Most software developers, therefore, include one or more batch files that make the installation process much easier for users.

The AUTOEXEC.BAT File The most commonly used batch file is a special one named AUTOEXEC.BAT–the auto-execute batch file. Whenever you boot up your computer, DOS searches the root directory of the current drive for this AUTOEXEC.BAT file. If there is no AUTOEXEC.BAT file present, DOS simply asks you to supply the current date and time, and then presents its prompt. If, on the other hand, AUTOEXEC.BAT is found, then that batch file is automatically executed. Since the AUTOEXEC.BAT file is automatically invoked every time you boot up your computer, it is ideal for listing any commands and programs you always run when you first turn on your machine. For example, if there is a subdirectory that you always use, you could put a CD (Change Directory) command in the AUTOEXEC.BAT to move into that subdirectory. Most DOS users eventually set up their own AUTOEXEC.BAT files or have someone else help them do so.

Conclusion

In this chapter of the *Software Guide*, you've learned several of the most frequently used DOS commands. To be sure, we haven't covered every DOS command or discussed every feature of this rich and powerful operating system. Most computer users, however, find that they primarily spend their time running application programs such as VP-Planner Plus. Their direct interaction with DOS is, for the most part, on the level of the commands and procedures we've introduced in this chapter. To learn even more about DOS, consult one of the many books completely devoted to the subject. Or, refer to the documentation provided by IBM and Microsoft: the *DOS User's Guide* and the *DOS Reference* manual.

Exercises

Multiple Choice

Choose the best selection to complete each statement.

_____________ 1. An operating system is a(n)
   a. hardware component of a mainframe computer system.
   b. application program that produces text files.
   c. set of programs that lets you use your computer's hardware and software resources.
   d. system of procedures for operating a computer.

_____________ 2. Transient routines or external commands are
   (a) kept in primary memory until the computer is shut off.
   (b) kept on disk and loaded into memory only when needed.
   (c) kept in ROM (read-only memory) chips.
   (d) used once then deleted.

_____________ 3. The driving force behind each new DOS release has usually been
   (a) the addition of a new disk drive capability.
   (b) an effort to improve the user interface.
   (c) an attempt to eliminate all bugs.
   (d) an effort by IBM and Microsoft to make more money.

_____________ 4. Upwardly compatible means that
   (a) you cannot take advantage of the new version's abilities.
   (b) all old software versions must be upgraded.
   (c) new hardware must be purchased to use the new version.
   (d) operations that worked with former versions work with the new version.

_____________ 5. A command is a(n)
   (a) combination of hardware switch settings.
   (b) operating system directive issued to a user.
   (c) application package instruction.
   (d) word or abbreviation that tells DOS to run a program.

_____________ 6. To boot DOS with the power off
   (a) insert the DOS disk and turn on the power.
   (b) hold down the Control, Alternate, and Delete keys at the same time.
   (c) turn the power on and issue the boot command.
   (d) turn the power on and kick the computer.

_____________ 7. Pressing Ctrl-Alt-Del will
   (a) invoke a DOS transient routine.
   (b) delete a file.
   (c) reboot DOS without having to shut off the computer.
   (d) execute an application program.

_____________ 8. The DOS directory command is
   (a) DIRECT.
   (b) LIST.
   (c) DIR.
   (d) CATALOG.

_____________ 9. The two parts of a DOS file name are
   (a) a disk drive designation and a disk sector number.
   (b) a primary file name and an optional extension.
   (c) a primary file name and a creation date.
   (d) a primary extension and the size in bytes.

____________ 10. Files with COM and EXE extensions usually designate
(a) external commands and executable program files.
(b) command files and extension files.
(c) configuration files and batch files.
(d) BASIC and FORTRAN files.

____________ 11. Pressing Ctrl-Num Lock or Pause will
(a) echo input and output to the printer.
(b) print the screen.
(c) cancel a command.
(d) temporarily halt screen scrolling.

____________ 12. To change the default disk drive
(a) put a new disk in drive A.
(b) type the new disk drive designation and press Enter.
(c) open up the computer and replace the faulty drive.
(d) issue the DIR command.

____________ 13. To display a disk and memory status report, enter
(a) status.
(b) dir.
(c) chkdsk.
(d) diskcopy.

____________ 14. Formatting a diskette does not
(a) check the diskette for bad sectors.
(b) wipe out all data on the diskette.
(c) mark off the space into sectors.
(d) sort files in the directory.

____________ 15. To format a system diskette you must
(a) reboot the system.
(b) use the /s parameter with the FORMAT command.
(c) enter the COPY command.
(d) purchase a master diskette from IBM.

____________ 16. One way to copy every file from disk drive A to B is to
(a) enter copy a:*.* b:.
(b) enter dir a: b:.
(c) enter copy a: b:.
(d) use the REN command.

____________ 17. To make an exact copy of an entire diskette, use
(a) COPY.
(b) DISKCOPY.
(c) DIR.
(d) Ctrl-Alt-Del.

____________ 18. Entering the command del *.* will
(a) reboot the system.
(b) copy all files to the disk in the default drive.
(c) rename all files on the disk in the default drive.
(d) erase all files from the disk in the default drive.

____________ 19. To display a text file on your screen use the
(a) PRINT command.
(b) DISKCOPY command.
(c) TYPE command.
(d) Ctrl-Num Lock key.

____________ 20. To run a program or batch file you must
(a) type its filename and press the Enter key.
(b) reboot DOS.
(c) press Ctrl-Break.
(d) first make a backup copy.

Fill-In

1. A disk operating system has many utilities for dealing with the ____________ that are stored on disks.

2. ____________ is usually used with IBM computers while ____________ is usually used with compatible computers such as those made by Compaq, AT&T, Tandy, and Zenith.

3. Booting DOS refers to the process of loading the disk operating system into ________________.

4. In many cases, when you first boot DOS it asks you to enter the ________________ and the ________________.

5. The ________________ command can be used to list the names, sizes, and creation dates and times of all the files on a disk.

6. A file's primary filename can have from one to ________________ characters in it.

7. File name extensions are often used to ________________ files.

8. You can press the ________________ key to cancel a command if you haven't pressed the Enter key yet.

9. You can press ________________ to cancel a command before it finishes normally.

10. The DOS ________________ indicates the current default disk drive.

11. The ________________ command can tell you how much memory is installed in your computer.

12. A diskette must be ________________ before it can be used to store program and data files.

13. The ________________ command can be used to duplicate one or more files on the same or on different disks.

14. ________________ file name characters can be used to refer to several files at the same time.

15. The DISKCOPY command will automatically ________________ the target diskette if it's brand new.

16. The REN command can be used to ________________ one or more file names.

17. To remove a file from a disk, you would enter ________________ or ________________ followed by the file's name.

18. The TYPE command lets you display ________________ files on your screen.

19. You could use the ________________ command to produce a hard copy of a text file.

20. The DOS commands used to create, change to, and remove subdirectories are ________________, ________________, and ________________.

Short Problems

1. If you have access to a diskette other than the DOS floppies, produce a directory listing of the files on it. If you have a printer, try using Ctrl-PrtSc to turn on printer echoing before you issue the directory command so that you can get a hard copy.

2. When you booted DOS, you were asked to supply the date and time. Two DOS commands, DATE and TIME, tell you the current date and time and let you change these settings. Try the DATE and TIME commands. If you don't want to change the date and time settings, just press the **Enter** key when asked for the new date or time. Notice how DOS automatically figures out and displays the day of the week.

3. Use the * global file name character to produce a directory listing of all the files on the DOS Startup disk with an EXE extension.

4. Use the * global file name character to produce a directory listing of all the files on the DOS Startup disk whose names begin with the letter K.

5. Use the ? global file name character to produce a directory listing of all the files on the DOS Startup disk that have an E as the second letter of their primary filenames.

6. You've probably noticed the "Volume in drive A has no label" message DOS gives when it displays a directory of the DOS disk. The FORMAT command has an option that lets you specify a name for a disk, or volume label as DOS calls it. Try formatting a blank disk with this command:

   format b:/v

   If you have only one floppy drive, enter this instead:

   format a:/v

   The /V is an optional parameter that tells the FORMAT command to ask you for a volume label. Think up a name of 11 characters or less and enter it when FORMAT tells you to. When you're done, check the disk's directory to see your volume label displayed.

7. DOS versions 3.0 and newer have a command that lets you supply or change a volume label without having to reformat a disk. If you have DOS 3.0 or newer try using the LABEL command on the new disk you've just formatted. Note that you can't change the label of the original DOS disk because it's write-protected.

8. If you don't know what DOS version you have, enter **ver**. This command displays the number of the DOS version you are using.

9. Another way to find out the volume label of a disk is to use the VOL command. Enter **vol a:**. This command displays the volume label (if there is one) of the disk in drive A.

10. It is possible to display a text file on your screen by using the COPY command instead of the TYPE command. In certain cases, DOS can refer to its peripheral devices as if they were files. There are several file names that have a special meaning to DOS. These are called DOS device names. For example, CON refers to the console, or the keyboard and screen. Put the disk with your README.TXT file in drive A and enter this command:

    copy readme.txt con

    You should see the text of file README.TXT displayed on your screen just as if you used the TYPE command.

11. Just as CON is a DOS device name that refers to the keyboard and screen, PRN is a DOS device name that refers to the printer. Try using the COPY command to get a printout of the README.TXT file.

12. The DIR command has two optional parameters that can be useful when looking at disks with lots of files on them. The /P parameter will automatically pause the display when the screen is full and let you press a key to continue. The /W parameter will display the directory in a wide format across the screen, omitting the sizes and creation dates and times so that more file names will fit at once. Put your DOS Startup disk in drive A and try entering these options:

    dir /p
    dir /w

3

Spreadsheets: VP-Planner Plus

Learning Objectives

By the end of this chapter, you should be able to do the following:

- Invoke the VP-Planner Plus program
- Move around a VP-Planner Plus spreadsheet
- Enter numbers, labels, and formulas into a spreadsheet
- Edit previously entered data
- Use the VP-Planner Plus command menus
- Design the format of a spreadsheet
- Complete a spreadsheet
- Save a spreadsheet in disk storage
- Print a spreadsheet
- Retrieve an existing spreadsheet from disk storage
- Modify an existing spreadsheet
- Use VP-Planner Plus formulas
- Use VP-Planner Plus functions
- Use VP-Planner Plus macros
- Create, save, and print a graph

Introduction

Electronic spreadsheet software is undoubtedly one of the most popular and useful of all microcomputer applications on the market today. Adaptable to all kinds of tasks from accounting chores to games, electronic spreadsheet programs are commonly found in businesses, schools, offices, and homes. In fact, this type of software has significantly contributed to the personal computer boom; many people have purchased microcomputer systems just so they can run a particular spreadsheet package. In this chapter we'll be introducing VP-Planner Plus, a powerful yet flexible tool that can be applied to a wide range of common problems.

An electronic spreadsheet is like a conventional paper spreadsheet in that it's a table consisting of columns and rows of entries. These rows and columns can be easily manipulated and set up so that calculations can be performed on them. A great advantage to electronic spreadsheet programs is that if you make a change in one place, all other dependent figures are automatically recalculated.

This automatic recalculation makes it a simple matter to correct mistakes quickly, update values, and try out any number of "what if" hypotheses without having to perform repetitious manual calculations. Most people find spreadsheet programs easy to learn and straightforward to use.

General Features of VP-Planner Plus

Although VP-Planner Plus has an impressive set of sophisticated features, it's rather easy for beginners to learn to use on a more modest level. In this chapter we'll concentrate on VP-Planner Plus's most commonly used features. Some of the things you can do with VP-Planner Plus include:

- **Moving Around the Spreadsheet** VP-Planner Plus makes it easy to move to any position in a spreadsheet. You can use arrow keys to move row by row or column by column, or you can use other keystrokes and commands to move more rapidly.
- **Entering Data** You can enter into a spreadsheet three basic kinds of data: labels, numbers, and formulas.
- **Editing Data** Once data have been entered into a spreadsheet, you can correct errors, make modifications, or update values without having to retype entire entries.
- **Using Menus** VP-Planner Plus has an excellent system of menus for selecting commands and options. You can highlight an item or press its first letter to make a choice.
- **Designing Spreadsheet Formats** You can use VP-Planner Plus to design custom spreadsheets because the program enables you to set column widths, control the format of displayed numbers, and enter titles, headings, and labels.
- **Saving Spreadsheets in Disk Storage** When completed, spreadsheets can be kept in disk files for later reference, updating, or printing.
- **Printing Spreadsheets** Entire spreadsheets or just specified portions can be output to a printer to create reports.
- **Retrieving Spreadsheets** Previously saved spreadsheets can be loaded from disk storage into primary memory where you can work on them with VP-Planner Plus.
- **Modifying Spreadsheets** Existing spreadsheets can be altered to correct errors, update values, or try out "what if" hypotheses.
- **Using Formulas** VP-Planner Plus lets you construct formulas to compute numeric values, manipulate labels, and compare entries.
- **Using Functions** The VP-Planner Plus program provides a rich set of built-in functions that you can use in your formulas. These functions include common mathematical, statistical, financial, and logical operations. There are even functions that let you work with dates and times.
- **Using Macros** Repetitive operations can be automated through the use of VP-Planner Plus macros, which let you store and replay keystrokes.
- **Creating Graphs** VP-Planner Plus lets you extract data from your spreadsheets and display these in any of several different kinds of graphs. Once created, graphs can also be saved and later printed.

Getting Started

Although VP-Planner Plus is a powerful application package, it's fairly easy to use. It is a straightforward program and has extensive help facilities built right in. The package comes on two 5¼-inch diskettes: the Program Disk and the Sample Files

Disk. The three most likely arrangements for students running VP-Planner Plus are:

1. on a computer with one or two floppy drives and the VP-Planner Plus program on the Program Disk
2. on a computer with a hard disk and at least one floppy drive and the VP-Planner Plus program on the hard disk
3. on a computer connected to a local area network and the VP-Planner Plus program installed on the network's disk server

In each of these cases the computer may be any IBM-compatible microcomputer. Because there are so many different ways to organize computers, your instructor might have you initially follow some simple directions unique to your particular installation. Once you're situated, however, you should be able to work the following lessons as they're described.

Lesson 1: Running VP-Planner Plus

Like any application package, VP-Planner Plus must be loaded into your computer's memory before you can use it. So, the first thing to do is access and execute the VP-Planner Plus program.

Step 1: Boot Up DOS

If your computer isn't already turned on and running DOS, you'll need to boot up. For computer systems with one or two floppy drives, put your DOS disk in drive A, close the door, and turn on the system unit. If your computer has a hard disk or is connected to a local area network, just turn it on. If your display is a color monitor (with three knobs on the front), turn it on by twisting the top knob. Turn on your printer, if you have one. Finally, enter the date and time to complete the DOS boot-up process as we described in Lesson 1 of Chapter 2.

Step 2: Insert VP-Planner Plus Program Disk or Switch to the VP-Planner Plus Subdirectory

If you're going to run VP-Planner Plus from a floppy, you'll need a copy of the Program Disk. For one-floppy systems, remove the DOS disk from drive A and replace it with your VP-Planner Plus Program Disk. If your computer has two floppy drives, just put the VP-Planner Plus Program Disk in drive B, close the door, and enter **b:**. Another possibility for two-floppy systems is to remove the DOS disk from drive A, replace it with your VP-Planner Plus Program Disk, and put a formatted diskette in drive B to hold your worksheet files.

If you're using a hard disk or network, you may need to follow some other directions from your instructor in order to access VP-Planner Plus. For example, on a hard disk system, you may need to first switch to the VP-Planner Plus subdirectory by entering **cd \vpp**.

Step 3: Invoke VP-Planner Plus

Once you get situated in the proper disk drive and directory, running VP-Planner Plus is easy. Type **vpp** and press **Enter** to invoke the program. The disk drive access light will go on as VP-Planner Plus is loaded into your computer's primary memory. The screen will momentarily blank and then you'll see the copyright screen shown in Figure 3.1

This screen will remain for several seconds while the program is loading. It shows the VP-Planner Plus logo, copyright dates, and whether it is licensed for an individual or a group of people. When VP-Planner Plus is finished being loaded into memory, a horizontal and a vertical bar appear on the screen. The identification screen will disappear when the first key stroke is made.

Figure 3.1 VP-Planner Plus Copyright Screen

```
                V P - P l a n n e r    P L U S

               Copyright 1985, 1986, 1987, 1988
        James Stephenson, David Mitchell, Kent Brothers
        Stephenson Software Inc. -- All rights reserved

           Published by Paperback Software International
```

Lesson 2: Exploring the VP-Planner Plus Worksheet

An electronic spreadsheet program like VP-Planner Plus configures the computer's memory so that the screen resembles a columnar pad of rows and columns. Because this configuration dynamically exists in the computer's memory, it can be much larger than an ordinary paper pad. In fact, it's usually too large to even fit completely on the computer screen all at once. So, VP-Planner Plus gives you a movable window into this large, conceptual spreadsheet. This window is known as the VP-Planner Plus worksheet. Since *worksheet* is the term Paperback Software International uses in its documentation, for the rest of this manual we'll use the terms *worksheet* and *spreadsheet* interchangeably.

Step 1: Examine the Worksheet Display

Press the **Enter** key to get rid of the copyright screen. VP-Planner Plus presents you with the blank worksheet shown in Figure 3.2.

The most obvious parts of this display are the highlighted horizontal and vertical borders. The letters along the top designate columns, and the numbers down the left edge designate rows. Although you can see only 8 columns and 20 rows at the moment, the whole worksheet is really much larger than this. Imagine the

Figure 3.2 Blank VP-Planner Plus Worksheet

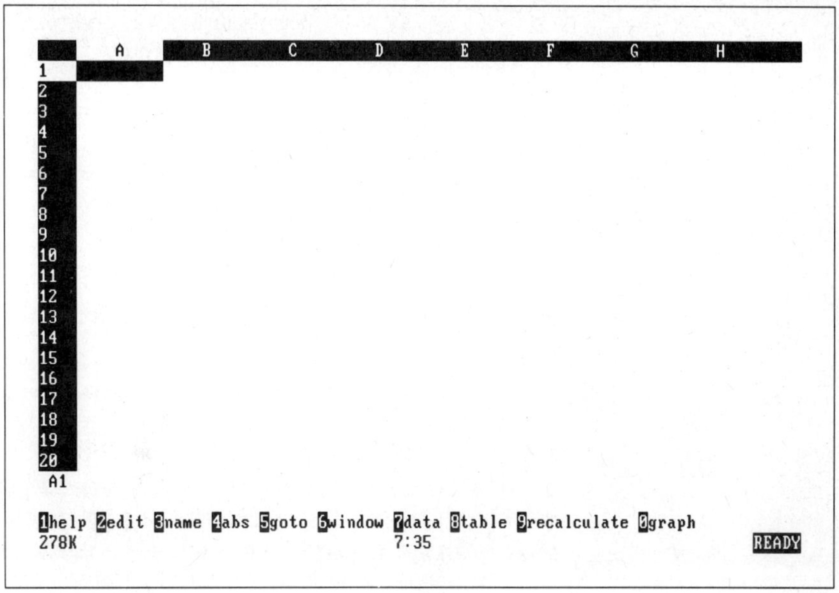

columns continuing out beyond the right edge of the screen and the rows continuing down below the bottom. VP-Planner Plus gives you a maximum of 256 columns and 9,999 rows. The columns are lettered starting with A to Z, then AA to AZ, BA to BZ, and so on up to IV. The rows are simply numbered 1 to 9,999.

Each intersection of a column and a row is called a cell. A **cell** is the basic unit of storage in a worksheet—where you put numbers, text, and computational formulas. Each cell is identified and located by its column letter(s) and row number. For example, A1 refers to the cell located at the intersection of the first column and first row. This column-row designation is known as the **cell address** because it uniquely identifies and locates each storage unit.

Because there are a maximum of 256 columns and 9,999 rows, the total number of cells is 256 × 9,999, or 2,559,744. However, this statement is a bit misleading. Although VP-Planner Plus can address all those cells, you can't actually fill every single cell on a standard PC. Cells don't use memory until you put something in them. A standard IBM PC (without an expanded memory board) can have up to 640K (655,360) bytes of primary memory. Even if you put only a single byte in each cell, you obviously can't fill over 2 million cells if you have only 640K of memory. In other words, the maximum size of a filled worksheet is dependent on the amount of memory installed in your computer.

As you can see, the worksheet area is completely blank except for a highlighted bar in cell A1. The column letter and row number where the cell pointer is currently located are not highlighted so you can tell at a glance where you are. The highlighted bar, known as the **cell pointer**, marks your current location within the worksheet. The cell pointer is always superimposed on the current cell—the place in the worksheet where you can enter data or initiate commands.

The space at the very bottom of your screen is known as the **control panel**. These four lines are used to display information, messages, menu choices, and prompts. The line immediately below row 20 shows the address and contents of the current cell. So, the *A1* indicates that the cell pointer is currently at cell A1. The blank line underneath the A1 shows that the current cell has nothing stored in it at the moment. The next line shows the menu of VP-Planner Plus commands that you can invoke using the function keys. They'll become more meaningful to you as you learn how to use them in later lessons.

Finally, at the bottom left of the worksheet screen, the amount of available memory is displayed. The middle of this line shows the time based on what you entered when you booted up DOS or the time supplied to DOS by your computer's internal battery-operated clock. The highlighted block in the lower right corner is VP-Planner Plus's mode indicator. It describes the current mode of operation. At this time the mode indicator displays READY, telling you that VP-Planner Plus is simply waiting for you to enter data or execute a command.

Step 2: Move Around the Worksheet

The VP-Planner Plus program lets you easily move the cell pointer to any of the over 2 million cells it can address. You can execute a move in several ways. Probably the most straightforward method is with the arrow keys. Pressing one of the Up, Down, Left, or Right Arrow keys on the right side of your keyboard will move the cell pointer in that direction. If you hit the edge of the worksheet, however, the cell pointer won't move and VP-Planner Plus will just beep. Press the **Right Arrow** key three times. See how the cell pointer moves to column D1 and the cell address in the control panel changes accordingly. Now try the **Down Arrow** key three times. The cell pointer should now be at D4. Press the **Right Arrow** key again, but this time keep holding it down for several seconds. Your keyboard's typematic feature will automatically send repeated keystrokes to VP-Planner Plus and the cell pointer will rapidly travel to the right. As the cell pointer hits the edge of the screen, the worksheet will also scroll to the right, revealing more columns. Now hold down the **Down Arrow** key and watch the worksheet scroll down. Try going back up to the top or over to the left as far as you can go. You'll know when you get there, because VP-Planner Plus will beep each time it receives a keystroke that attempts to move the cell pointer past an edge of the worksheet.

Step 3: Jump Around the Worksheet

The VP-Planner Plus program offers other ways to move around within a worksheet that are more rapid than holding down an arrow key. Here are some keys you should try:

Home	Always returns the cell pointer to A1
Page Up	Moves the cell pointer up one whole screen
Page Down	Moves the cell pointer down one whole screen
Tab	Moves the cell pointer one screen to the right
Shift-Tab	Moves the cell pointer one screen to the left

Press **End**, release it, and then press the **Up Arrow** key
Moves the cell pointer to the nonblank cell above or the top edge

Press **End**, release it, and then press the **Down Arrow** key
Moves the cell pointer to the nonblank cell below or the bottom edge

Press **End**, release it, and then press the **Left Arrow** key
Moves the cell pointer to the next nonblank cell to the left or the left edge

Press **End**, release it, and then press the **Right Arrow** key
Moves the cell pointer to the next nonblank cell to the right or the right edge

Step 4: Move to a Particular Cell

The program VP-Planner Plus also provides an easy way to move the cell pointer to an explicit address. Press the **F5** key. This key invokes VP-Planner Plus's "Go

To" procedure that lets you specify the address of the cell you want to move the cell pointer to. If you're currently at cell A1, VP-Planner Plus will ask you to:

```
Enter destination cell: A1
```

The program initially suggests your current location as the address of the destination cell. To move the cell pointer to J34, just type **j34** and press **Enter**. Note that it doesn't matter if you type the column letters of cell addresses in lowercase or uppercase.

Lesson 3: Entering Data

Besides moving the cell pointer around, there's not much you can do with an empty worksheet. VP-Planner Plus is, after all, a tool for entering, storing, manipulating, and presenting data. In the context of VP-Planner Plus, the term **data** refers to what you can enter into a cell and is categorized into three types:

- **Numbers** Numeric quantities
- **Labels** Any kind of text, like headings
- **Formulas** Computational expressions

Let's begin by filling up a few of those empty cells with data.

Step 1: Move the Cell Pointer

The first thing you must do when entering data into a worksheet is move the cell pointer to the cell where the item is to go. It doesn't matter to VP-Planner Plus where you put data; any cell can contain any type of data. Your main concern in choosing a cell in which to enter a particular data item is how you want to organize your worksheet. You need to plan out, at least in your mind, how you want the final worksheet to look. Then you can reserve certain rows or columns for labels and headings, and decide how many rows and columns you need for your figures. Let's start with a small, simple worksheet. As we go through subsequent lessons, we'll add to it and modify it. Ultimately, you'll wind up with a worksheet that exemplifies those used in many business applications. For now, let us do the planning; we'll tell you what to put where. When you're done with the following lessons, you'll have plenty of opportunity to plan and set up your own worksheets in the exercises at the end of this chapter.

Use the **Arrow** keys or the **F5** key to move the cell pointer to A14. For now, this is where you'll begin. We've had you leave room for some headings that will be added later.

Step 2: Enter Labels

Anything you enter that doesn't look like a number or formula is assumed by VP-Planner Plus to be a **label**. To be more precise, a label is really any text that doesn't begin with one of the following characters:

0 1 2 3 4 5 6 7 8 9 . + – ($ # @

If you have a label that you want to begin with one of these characters (like an address, Social Security number, phone number, and so on), you can precede it with a single quote ('). This symbol tells VP-Planner Plus to treat the characters that follow the quote as a label, not as a number or formula. In VP-Planner Plus the single quote is called a **label-prefix character**; we'll have more to say about this and other label-prefix characters in a later lesson in this chapter.

To enter a label, simply type its characters and press **Enter** when you're done. For example, with the cell pointer at A14, type **Sales Income**. Notice how the Function menu line disappeared, a cursor appeared in the control panel and how the mode indicator changed to say LABEL. When you enter data, you'll see that they first appear on the second line of the control panel. The data aren't actually stored in the current cell until you press Enter. If you make a mistake before you press Enter, you can use the Backspace key to erase what you've done and type it again. Try backspacing over *Income* and then type it again. When you're sure you've typed **Sales Income** correctly, press **Enter**. Your screen should look like Figure 3.3.

Figure 3.3 Sales Income Label Entered at Cell A14

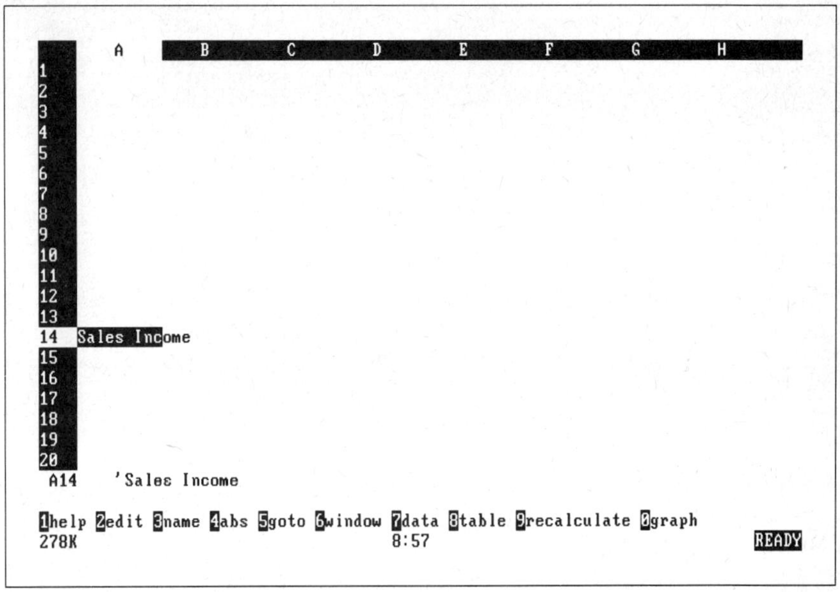

The top line of the control panel shows that the current cell is A14 and the contents of that cell is *'Sales Income*. Even though you didn't type it, VP-Planner Plus automatically added the single quote label-prefix character. Now look in the worksheet. See how the label-prefix character isn't displayed in the actual worksheet area. Also notice how the label overflows the cell pointer. By default, the width of VP-Planner Plus cells is nine characters. We'll show you later how to change the width of a column of cells, but for now it doesn't matter that the label is wider than the cell. This disparity happens quite often in VP-Planner Plus and causes no problems if the cell to the right is empty. In fact, VP-Planner Plus can hold up to 240 characters in a cell. Even if the cell to the right isn't empty, VP-Planner Plus stores the entire label you typed; it just doesn't display the part that overflows unless the cell to the right is empty.

To continue, press the **Down Arrow** key to move the cell pointer to A15 and type **Labor Income**, but this time press the **Down Arrow** key instead of Enter. Although we said before to press Enter to store an item in a cell when you're done typing it, any of the cell pointer movement keys will also work. This alternative is handy if you're going to enter an item in one cell and then immediately move to an adjacent cell to enter another item. Instead of pressing Enter and then Down Arrow, all you have to do is press Down Arrow by itself. Now that you're already in cell A16, type **Total** and press **Enter**.

Step 3: Enter Numbers

Entering numbers is just like entering labels; all you do is type them and press Enter. As far as VP-Planner Plus is concerned, a **number** is any entry that begins with one of these characters:

0 1 2 3 4 5 6 7 8 9 . + – $ (

You may enter numbers without decimal points (like 10, –22, or 1234) or with decimal points (like .5, –0.12, or 11.123). Don't include spaces or commas in a number. When you enter a number, you may precede it with + or $, or enclose it in parentheses, but these characters won't be displayed in the worksheet. In addition to normal decimal notation, you can also enter numbers in scientific notation. For example, 4.32E+05 (which equals 432,000) and –2.54E-5 (which equals –0.0000254) are both valid VP-Planner Plus number entries. This capability lets you include very large and very small numbers in your worksheet. VP-Planner Plus also lets you enter a number as a percentage. It automatically converts the percentage to decimal notation.

As you can see, the program makes a distinction between the actual numerical value and the format in which that numerical value is displayed in the worksheet. VP-Planner Plus gives you considerable control over that format. We'll be covering some of these issues in a later lesson in this chapter. For example, you can specify that commas are to be used to separate thousands, how many decimal places to display, whether to precede numbers with dollar signs, and so on.

To enter a couple of numbers into your worksheet, move the cell pointer to C14. Type **10563.5** and press the **Down Arrow** key. Notice how the mode indicator changes to say VALUE while you enter a numeric value. Now type **7987.25** into cell C15 and press the **Down Arrow** key again. By default, VP-Planner Plus displays only as many decimal places as it needs to and it right-justifies numbers within cells.

Step 4: Enter a Formula

In order to tell VP-Planner Plus to do something with the numbers you enter, you need formulas. A **formula** is an instruction that tells VP-Planner Plus to perform some calculations. The formula can include numbers, arithmetic operators (like + and –), cell addresses, and functions. We'll have more to say about functions and the other arithmetic operators later. For now, type **+C14+C15** into cell C16 and press **Enter**. Figure 3.4 shows what you should see.

The formula you've just entered instructs VP-Planner Plus to take the number stored in cell C14, add it to the number in cell C15, and display the result in C16. The most important fact to notice here is that the cell addresses in this formula are like variables in an algebraic expression: no matter what values are currently stored in cells C14 and C15, cell C16 will always display their sum. Another important concept to understand is that what's stored in cell C16 is the formula *+C14+C15* not the number *18550.75*. You know this because the entry in the control panel reads *+C14+C15*, while what you see in cell C16 is *18550.75*. The number displayed is just what results from computing the formula. Finally, you might be wondering why the formula begins with a plus sign. The reason is that a VP-Planner Plus formula must begin with one of these characters:

0 1 2 3 4 5 6 7 8 9 . + – (@ # $

Figure 3.4 Formula +C14+C15 Entered

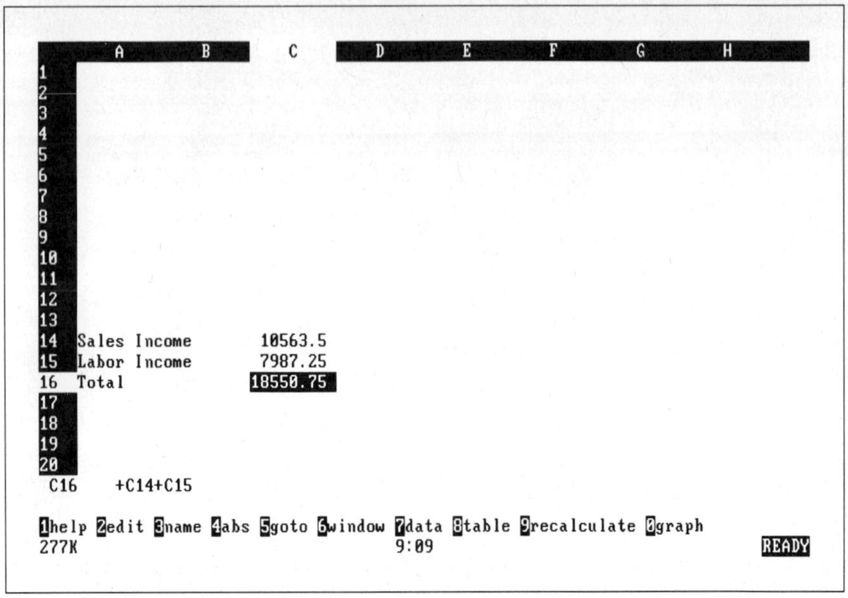

The cell address C14 begins with a C; if you don't put something in front to tell VP-Planner Plus that what follows is a formula, it will assume the entry is a label and won't do the calculation. The unary plus sign in front of the first cell address doesn't change the value of the result in any way, but it does enable VP-Planner Plus to recognize the entry as a formula.

Lesson 4: Editing Data

What happens if you make an error typing a data item but don't discover it until after you've pressed Enter? Or what if you want to go back and update or modify the existing contents of a cell? Fortunately, VP-Planner Plus provides ways of editing data you've already entered.

Step 1: Move the Cell Pointer

Just as when you were entering data, you must position the cell pointer at the cell with which you want to work. Let's change the label in cell A16 to *Total Income*. Move the cell pointer there with the **Arrow** keys or by pressing **F5**.

Step 2: Retype the Entry

The simplest way to edit the data in a cell is just to retype it. If there's already something in a cell and you move to that cell and enter something else, VP-Planner Plus will replace the old contents with the new entry. For example, with A16 as your current cell, type **Total Income** and press **Enter**. The VP-Planner Plus program will replace the *Total* with *Total Income*.

Step 3: Use the EDIT Mode

If an existing entry is long or complex and you don't need to change the whole thing, retyping the entire entry can be time consuming and error prone. Fortunately, VP-Planner Plus also has a method by which you can change only part of a cell's existing contents.

To edit a completed entry, first move the cell pointer to the cell in which it's stored. For example, let's edit the sales income figure, so move the cell pointer to C14. To invoke VP-Planner Plus's EDIT mode, press **F2**. The mode indicator will change to EDIT, the contents of the current cell will appear in the second line of the control panel, and the cursor will be placed at the end of the entry (see Figure 3.5). Use the Left and Right Arrow keys to move the cursor within the entry to any character you want to change. For example, to change the *6* to a *2,* press the **Left Arrow** key four times to move the cursor beneath the *6*. Now press **Insert** to turn insert mode off and type **2.** Just like many word processing programs, VP-Planner Plus has an insert/overtype mode that's toggled by pressing the Insert key. By default, insert mode is turned on, which means that new characters will be inserted into entries when you type in EDIT mode. When you're done editing the entry, just press **Enter** to store it in the cell. As you do this, watch the total income figure. You'll see that it's automatically recalculated to reflect the new value in cell C14. This recalculation occurs because the formula in cell C16 is based on the contents of cell C14, the one you've just edited.

Figure 3.5 Editing Cell C14

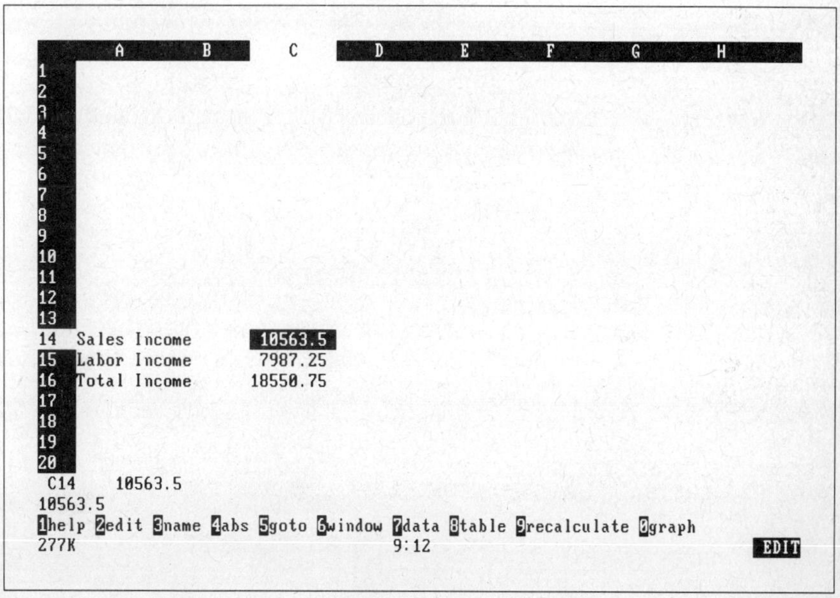

As you've just seen, some keys work differently when you're in EDIT mode than when you're in READY, LABEL, or VALUE mode. Here's a brief summary of the keys and the actions they perform when you're in VP-Planner Plus's EDIT mode:

Enter	Stores the entry and returns to READY mode
Backspace	Erases the character to the cursor's left
Delete	Erases the character at the cursor
Escape	Clears the second line of the control panel
Insert	Toggles the character insert/overwrite mode

Home or **Ctrl-Right Arrow**	Moves to the first character of the entry
End or **Ctrl-Left Arrow**	Moves to the last character of the entry
Left Arrow	Moves the cursor one character to the left
Right Arrow	Moves the cursor one character to the right
Up Arrow	Stores the entry and moves up one cell
Down Arrow	Stores the entry and moves down one cell
Page Up	Stores the entry and moves up one screen
Page Down	Stores the entry and moves down one screen

Lesson 5: Exploring the VP-Planner Plus Command Menus

So far, you've learned how to enter and edit data items in worksheet cells. As fundamental and important as these operations are, you've barely begun to scratch the surface of VP-Planner Plus's capabilities until you learn how to use commands. Commands are the means by which you work with, rearrange, and otherwise manipulate the data stored in worksheet cells. In addition, you use commands to control the appearance, disk storage, and output of VP-Planner Plus worksheets. Menus are the way you select and execute VP-Planner Plus commands. This lesson will briefly introduce VP-Planner Plus command menus. Later lessons will cover in greater detail some of the most important commands as you actually try them out.

Step 1: Display the Main Menu

Press / (Forward Slash) to display the main VP-Planner Plus menu of commands on your screen. Figure 3.6 shows what you should see.

Figure 3.6 Main VP-Planner Plus Menu of Commands

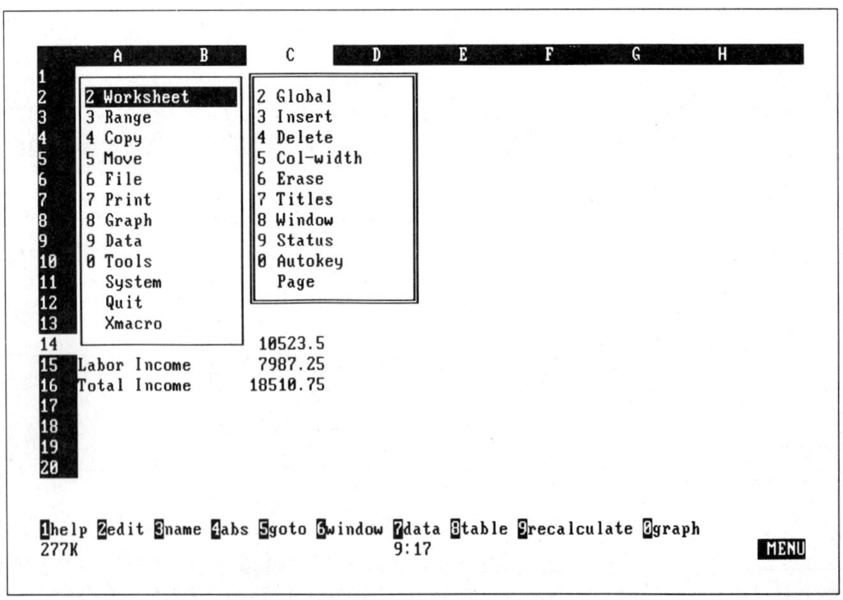

The mode indicator now says MENU. The left-most box is the Main menu. The highlighted block shows the command that will be invoked if you press Enter. The box to the right displays information relevant to the highlighted command. In many cases this information will be a list of additional options available to you when you invoke the highlighted command. For example, Worksheet is the command currently highlighted; if you press Enter, VP-Planner Plus overlays the Main menu with the submenu and displays a third box, again displaying information relevant to the highlighted command. In this case, the third box contains commands relevant to the Worksheet Global command.

Step 2: Move the Highlighted Block

Selecting a command or option from a VP-Planner Plus menu is really quite easy. To move the highlighted block, simply press the Up or Down Arrow key. Try it now by pressing the **Down Arrow** key. See how the second box changes each time you move the block. When you reach the end of the command list, press the **Down Arrow** key again and the highlighted block will wrap around to the beginning again. Now repeatedly press the **Up Arrow** key to see that you can move backward too.

Step 3: Select a Command from the Menu

There are three ways to select an option from a VP-Planner Plus menu. The first is to position the highlighted block on the option and press Enter. The second way is to press the key of the first letter of the option's name. VP-Planner Plus menus are carefully designed so that each command or option choice in any given list begins with a different letter. The third way is to press the function key corresponding to the number next to the menu option. For example, to select the Worksheet command from the Main menu, you can either position the highlighted block on the command and press **Enter**, simply type **W** (or **w**), or press **F2**. Try one of these methods now to select Worksheet. Your screen will look like Figure 3.7.

Figure 3.7 Selecting Worksheet from the Main Menu

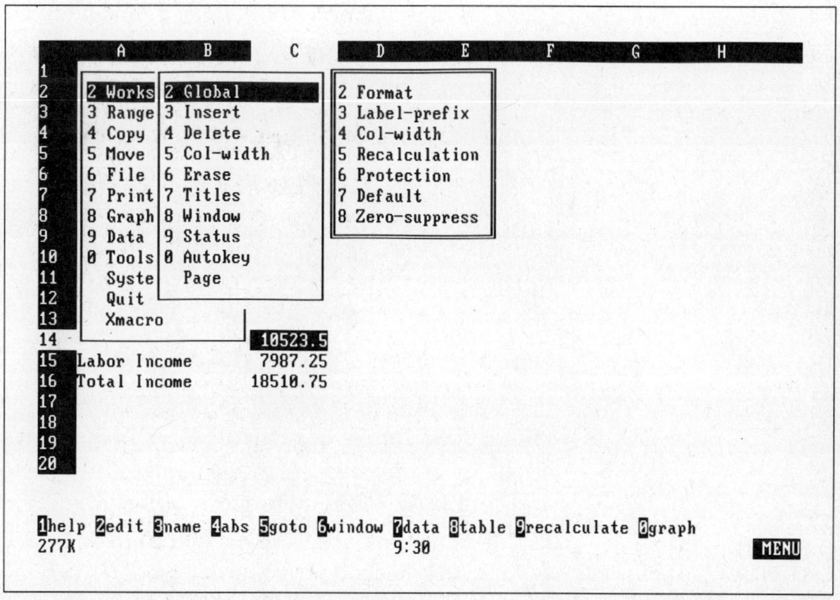

Step 4: Return from a Menu

Most of the time you can return to a previous menu without actually doing anything. For example, now that you've selected the Worksheet command you're in a submenu of options that lets you change certain worksheet settings. To return from this submenu to the Main menu, press **Escape**. You should now see the Main menu and the first level of submenus again. To return from the Main menu and go back to READY mode, press **Escape** again; the Main menu will disappear. Remember: when in doubt, you can usually return from the menu you're in by pressing Escape one or more times.

Step 5: Examine the Worksheet Command

Before we go on to construct a more substantial worksheet, let's quickly go through the Main menu commands and briefly describe what each one allows you to do. If you're not already looking at the Main menu, press / to display it on your screen. Highlight the Worksheet command if it isn't already highlighted and press **Enter**, type **w**, or press **F2**. As we go through each command option, follow along by highlighting it with the **Down Arrow** key. Be sure to read the submenu that pops up as you move the cell pointer.

The Worksheet options allow you to control the overall appearance of the worksheet, make major changes to its contents, control VP-Planner Plus's overall work methods, and change some disk directory and printer settings. Here's a quick summary of the Worksheet options:

Global Sets overall rules for processing the worksheet and establishes standard methods for communicating with printers and disks

Insert Inserts blank columns or rows into an existing worksheet

Delete Removes entire columns or rows from an existing worksheet

Col-width Sets the width of a single worksheet column

Erase Deletes the contents of all cells in the worksheet

Titles Freezes selected rows and/or columns so that they remain on the screen even if the worksheet is scrolled

Window Splits the display screen into as many as six screens to display different parts of the same worksheet at the same time

Status Displays the current global worksheet settings

Autokey Displays options for defining and using Autokey macros

Page Inserts above the current cell a page break that tells VP-Planner Plus to start a new page there when the worksheet is printed

Step 6: Examine the Range Command

Press **Escape** to get back to the Main menu and type **r** to select the Range command. The Range options allow you to perform operations on a rectangular block of one or more cells. A range can be a single cell, a row, a column, or several rows and columns. We'll have more to say about ranges and how to specify them later. For now, examine the list of Range options on your screen.

Format Sets the way in which numbers are to be displayed within a given range

Label	Sets the type of justification (left, right, center, or flush-right) for labels within a given range
Erase	Deletes the contents of a given range of cells
Name	Assigns a name to a given range so that it can be more easily referred to later
Justify	Reformats text within a column of cells so that each row conforms to a specified width
Protect	Disallows making any changes to a given range of cells
Unprot	Turns off a previous Range Protect command, allowing changes to be made again to a given range
Input	Limits the movement of the cell pointer to only unprotected cells within a given range
Col	Sets the column width for a range of cells
Value	Copies a range of cells, but for formulas copies only the values they evaluate to, not the formulas themselves
Transpose	Copies a column of cells to a row, or a row of cells to a column

Step 7: Examine the Copy Command

Press **Escape** to get back to the Main menu and press the **Down Arrow** key to move the highlight block to the Copy command. Don't press Enter to actually select the command because Copy doesn't have any submenu options to view. The Copy command allows you to copy a range of one or more cells to another range. This command is one of the most useful VP-Planner Plus commands because it can save you a considerable amount of repetitive typing. As you'll see later when you actually try it out, not only can the Copy command reproduce cell contents exactly, it can copy formulas and adjust any contained cell addresses accordingly.

Step 8: Examine the Move Command

Press the **Down Arrow** key again to highlight the Move command. This command is just like the Copy command, except that it erases the contents of the range you're moving from instead of just replicating it.

Step 9: Examine the File Command

Now type **f** to select the File command and examine the submenu. This important command allows you to transfer the contents of your worksheet back and forth between primary memory (where it resides when you're working on it with VP-Planner Plus) and more permanent disk storage. The File options are:

Retrieve	Loads a previously stored worksheet file from disk into primary memory where you can work on it with VP-Planner Plus
Save	Stores the current worksheet in a disk file so that you can retrieve it later
Combine	Incorporates all or just part of a worksheet file on disk into the worksheet currently in memory
Xtract	Stores a given range in a worksheet file on disk

Erase	Deletes files with the specified extension from disk storage
List	Displays a list of files with the specified extension currently on your disk
Import	Loads a data file created by some other program into primary memory, converting it into VP-Planner Plus format
Directory	Sets the current disk drive directory (the place in disk storage) where VP-Planner Plus will look for its files
Utility	Copies or renames a file currently stored on disk

Step 10: Examine the Print Command

Press **Escape** to return to the Main menu and use the **Down Arrow** key to highlight the Print command. This command has only two options. The first one lets you output your whole worksheet, or just a range, directly to your printer. If you don't have a printer attached to your computer or if you want to print the worksheet later with DOS, the Print command's second option lets you send the output to a print file with an extension of .PRN instead of directly to the printer.

Step 11: Examine the Graph Command

Press the **Down Arrow** key again to highlight the Graph command. If you are using a computer that has graphics capabilities, VP-Planner Plus can present line graphs, bar graphs, scatter plots, and pie charts. Graphs can be created based on the data in your worksheet and then saved on disk in a graph file to be displayed again later or printed.

Step 12: Examine the Data Command

Type **d** to select the Data command. This command provides you with some limited data management capabilities. Although VP-Planner Plus isn't a full-fledged data base management package, it does provide several very useful features. Since VP-Planner Plus is so flexible when it comes to the kinds of data that can be stored in worksheet cells, you can use it to set up and manage data in a tabular fashion. The options provided by the Data command are:

Fill	Fills a range with an ascending or descending sequence of numbers
Table	Creates a table of values to be used by formulas in certain types of calculations
Sort	Rearranges the rows of a worksheet in the order you specify
Query	Finds the rows of a worksheet that satisfy a given set of criteria
Distribution	Calculates the frequency distribution of a range of cells
External	Transfers data between the current worksheet and a data base file
Input	Enters data into a worksheet table from a data entry screen

Step 13: Examine the Tools Command

Press **Escape** to return to the Main menu and press the **Down Arrow** key to highlight the Tools command. This command makes word processor and graphics features available to enhance your worksheets. You can also choose to run another applications program, then return to the current worksheet.

Step 14: Examine the System Command

Press the **Down Arrow** key to highlight the System command. This command allows you to suspend VP-Planner Plus temporarily and go back to DOS. The feature is not the same as quitting, because VP-Planner Plus and your worksheet are kept in primary memory, in the background so to speak. When you're done with DOS, you can immediately return to what you were doing in VP-Planner Plus by typing **exit** at the DOS prompt and pressing **Enter**.

Step 15: Examine the Xmacro Command

Press the **Down Arrow** key twice to highlight the Xmacro command. (We'll skip the Quit command for the moment.) This command allows you to create and use **macros**, sequences of keystrokes that you can store and use to perform operations, repetitive procedures, and frequently used commands. We'll discuss macros in a later lesson.

Step 16: Examine the Quit Command

Finally, type **q** to select the Quit command. VP-Planner Plus will present you with two options: No and Yes. If you haven't saved your work yet, VP-Planner Plus tells you that the worksheet will be lost if you quit at this point. If you're really sure that you've saved your work and want to quit VP-Planner Plus, you would type **y** for yes. In this case, however, you're not done yet, so type **n** for no. The VP-Planner Plus program will return to READY mode.

Step 17: Explore the Help Facility

Fortunately for beginning users, VP-Planner Plus has one of the best help facilities in the software industry. It's like a concise reference manual that's always open to the right page. The F1 key calls up the VP-Planner Plus Help facility. If you are working on a hard disk, simply press **F1**. If you are working on a one or two floppy disk system, take out the disk in drive A, insert the Sample Files Disk, and press **F1**. The worksheet screen will clear and VP-Planner Plus will display information relevant to the command or operation with which you're currently working (see Figure 3.8). You can then press one of the keys listed along the bottom of the screen to display even more information. For example, press **F1** to select an index of Help screens if there's a particular topic about which you want to find out more. Spend some time exploring and become familiar with using the VP-Planner Plus Help screens. When you're done, press **Escape** to return to what you were doing before you pressed F1 (if you are working on a floppy disk system, replace the Sample Files Disk with the Program Disk that was in drive A before you pressed F1).

Figure 3.8 VP-Planner Plus's Help Facility

```
                              (5) Using Help

Help is always available.  Press <F1> at any time to see a help screen
relevant to the current mode or command.  For an index of all help topics,
press <F1> twice.

Many help screens include numbers enclosed in parentheses.  These are cross
references to other help screens. Cross references are also indicated at the
lower left of the screen.  To look at one of these references, press <F5>, type
the number, and press <ENTER>.

The lower right corner shows the next help screen.  To scan the next
screen, press <PGDN>.  For example, the topic of the next help screen after
this is "Ready Mode;" to view it, press <PGDN> or type <F5> 6 <ENTER>.

To return to previous screens you have viewed, press <PGUP> one or more
times.  To return to this screen from any other help screen, type
<F5> 5 <ENTER>.  To leave help, press <ESC>.

See also: (28) Function Keys

                                                  Next Screen:
                                                  (6) Ready Mode/Moving the Cursor/Quit
-----------------------------------------------------------------------------------------
        <F1> index   <PgDn> next   <PgUp> previous   <F5> goto   <ESC> exit
```

Lesson 6: Designing the Income Worksheet

Starting with this lesson, we're going to have you use VP-Planner Plus to construct a more substantial spreadsheet by adding more labels, numbers, and formulas to what you've already entered. The example we'll use is an income statement for a fictional locksmith business, shown in Figure 3.9. This example will be built around the spreadsheet you have already started.

Step 1: Set the Column Widths

As we mentioned before, the first step in building a spreadsheet is planning how you want it to look. In this case you already have an example to follow, so there's not much creative thought involved. If you were designing a spreadsheet from scratch, however, you'd have to consider its physical layout carefully. A good place to start when establishing a worksheet's format is setting appropriate column widths.

The default width of a column of cells in VP-Planner Plus is nine characters. Although this size is fine in many cases, it's frequently necessary to increase or decrease that width for certain columns. For the Kwik Key & Lock income statement, you'll need to set the width of column A to 16, B to 2, C to 10, and D through G to 11.

First, move the cell pointer to any cell in the column whose width is to be changed. To change the width of column A, press **Home** to move the cell pointer to A1. Now press **/** to display the Main menu, type **w** to select the Worksheet command, type **c** to choose the Col-width option, and type **s** (or press **Enter**) to set the width of the current column. VP-Planner Plus will display the following line in the control panel:

```
Enter desired column width (0-240): 9
```

Figure 3.9 Income Statement for Kwik Key & Lock

Kwik Key & Lock
1404 Silver Street
Urbana, Illinois 61801

YEARLY INCOME STATEMENT 1989

Item		Quarters				
		First	Second	Third	Fourth	Total
INCOME						
Sales Income	$	10,523.50	13,459.25	17,752.00	11,543.50	53,278.25
Labor Income	$	7,987.25	11,208.00	15,489.50	10,653.00	45,337.75
Total Income	$	18,510.75	24,667.25	33,241.50	22,196.50	98,616.00
EXPENSES						
Store Rental	$	1,500.00	1,500.00	1,500.00	1,500.00	6,000.00
Telephone	$	750.00	750.00	750.00	750.00	3,000.00
Utilities	$	450.00	450.00	450.00	450.00	1,800.00
Advertising	$	600.00	600.00	600.00	600.00	2,400.00
Insurance	$	250.00	250.00	250.00	250.00	1,000.00
Vehicles	$	750.00	1,200.50	1,087.25	1,345.20	4,382.95
Tax & Licenses	$	125.50	125.50	125.50	125.50	502.00
Tools	$	327.80	892.50	479.00	589.50	2,288.80
Office Supplies	$	213.50	186.75	300.89	288.00	989.14
Equipment	$	799.50	456.25	925.25	654.40	2,835.40
Accountant	$			350.00		350.00
Materials	$	2,500.50	2,785.75	3,111.25	2,354.20	10,751.70
Payroll	$	7,200.00	7,200.00	7,200.00	7,200.00	28,800.00
Misc. Services	$	258.00	129.50	321.70	150.50	859.70
Total Expenses	$	15,724.80	16,526.75	17,450.84	16,257.30	65,959.69
Depreciation	$	500.00	500.00	500.00	500.00	2,000.00
Bad Debts	$		159.20	213.13	25.60	397.93
Tot. Deductions	$	16,224.80	17,185.95	18,163.97	16,782.90	68,357.62
Net Profit	$	2,285.95	7,481.30	15,077.53	5,413.60	30,258.38

The current width of column A is 9, so that's what VP-Planner Plus will use if you don't enter anything else. As you can see, any number from 0 to 240 characters is an acceptable column width. To set the width of column A, type **16** and press **Enter**. Column A will widen accordingly, and VP-Planner Plus will return to READY mode. Now move the cell pointer to column B and repeat the process to set its width to 2, then set the width of column C to 10.

Now we want to set the widths of columns D through G. Move the cell pointer to D1. Call up the Main menu (press /), type **r** to select the Range command, type **c** to select the Col option, then type **s** or press **Enter** to set the column widths. In the second line of the control panel, VP-Planner Plus asks you to select the range of columns to be altered. Type **d1..g1** or press the **Right Arrow** three times to highlight those four columns and press **Enter**. From this point on, the procedure is the same as before. Enter **11** as the new column width for D through G. Your screen should look like Figure 3.10.

Step 2: Set the Number Display Format

As you can see from the small worksheet you've entered so far, by default VP-Planner Plus displays numbers without commas and with only as many decimal places as are necessary. For many worksheets that deal with dollar amounts, this format isn't appropriate. In the Kwik Key & Lock income statement worksheet we want two places to the right of each decimal point and commas separating thousands, like this: 10,523.50.

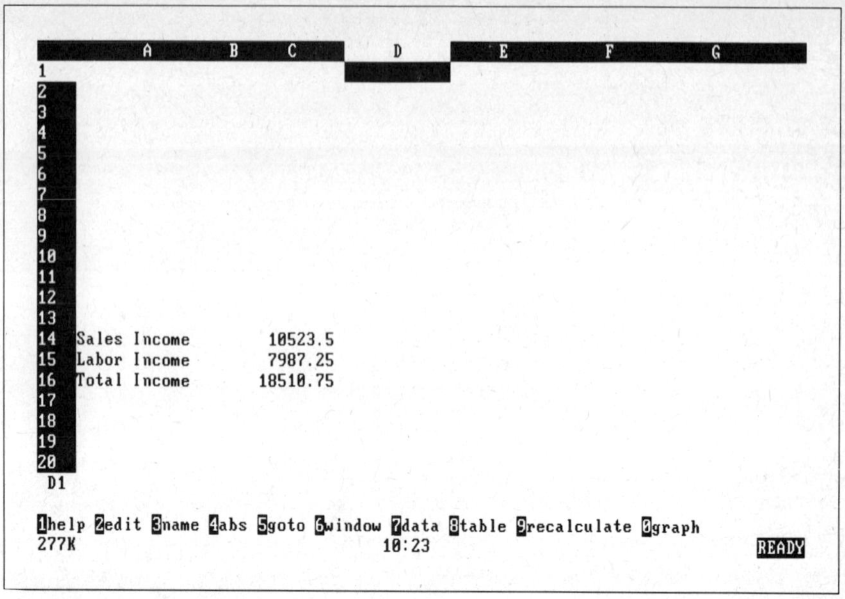

Figure 3.10 Changing the Column Widths

To change the number display format for the entire worksheet, press / to bring up the Main menu, type **w** to select the Worksheet command, type **g** to select the Global option, and type **f** to choose the Format option. VP-Planner Plus will display yet another list of options. Type **f** for Fixed to set the fixed number of decimal places to display. Type **2** and press **Enter**. Notice how the *10523.5* in cell C14 immediately changes to *10523.50*. Now type **/wgf** to get back into the global number format menu and press the **,** (comma) to specify that thousands are to be separated by commas. The VP-Planner Plus program will also ask you to enter the number of decimal places to display. Type **2** again and press **Enter**. The numbers in the worksheet should change accordingly, as shown in Figure 3.11.

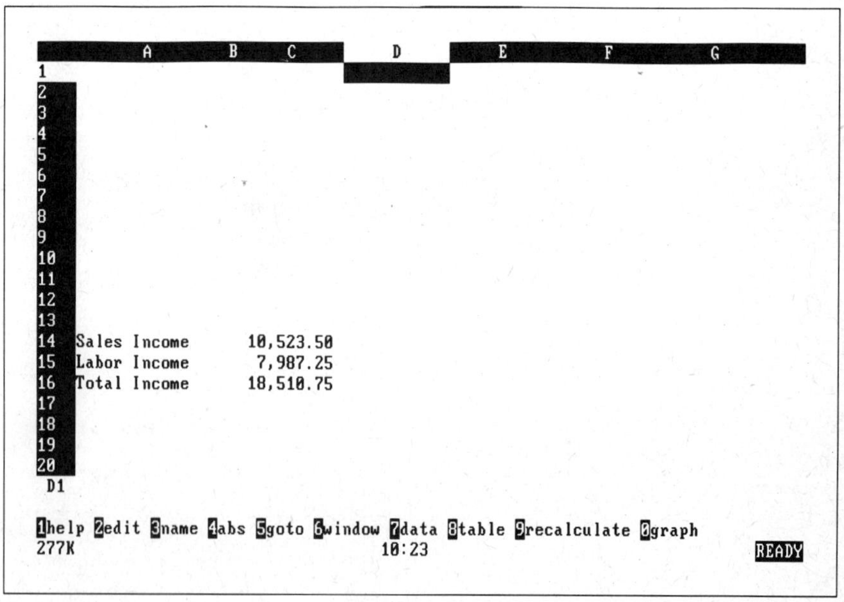

Figure 3.11 Setting the Number Display Format

Step 3: Enter Dividing Lines

The next step is to enter the dividing lines that will give the final worksheet its neat appearance. To enter the first line of asterisks (*), move the cell pointer to A1, type sixteen asterisks, and press **Enter**. A better way to fill the A1 cell with asterisks is to use the \ (Backward Slash) label-prefix character. When placed in front of a character, the \ tells VP-Planner Plus to repeat that character to fill the entire cell. To try it out, leave the cell pointer in A1, type *****, then press **Enter**. Notice how the entry in the control panel changes to *, but cell A1 is still filled with asterisks.

You could do this for each cell across the entire row, but the VP-Planner Plus Copy command can save you the trouble. As we said before, Copy can eliminate much repetitive typing by replicating the contents of one or more cells to a range of other cells. Type **/c** to select the Copy command. VP-Planner Plus will say:

```
Source cell range: A1..A1
```

Here the program's asking you what you want to copy. Unless you enter something else, VP-Planner Plus assumes that you want to copy the range consisting of only the current cell (A1..A1). In this case that's exactly what you want, so just press **Enter**. The VP-Planner Plus program will now ask:

```
Destination cell range: A1
```

You want VP-Planner Plus to copy the contents of cell A1 to cells B1, C1, D1, E1, F1, and G1. To designate this range, type **b1..g1**. Press **Enter** to have VP-Planner Plus complete the copy operation. You should see the entire first row of your worksheet fill with asterisks.

Now that you have a line of asterisks in row 1, you can copy the whole thing to enter the other line of asterisks in row 5. Type **/c** again to select the Copy command. This time, however, enter **a1..g1** for the source range and **a5..g5** for the destination range. The fifth row of your worksheet will fill with asterisks. Now use what you've learned to enter a line of equal signs (=) in rows 9, 12, and 41 and a line of dashes (—) in rows 17, 34, 37, and 39. Finally, enter the vertical bars (|) in B10 and B11, and the dollar signs ($) in cells B14..B16, B19..B33, B35, B36, B38, and B40. (NOTE: You'll have to precede each | and $ with the ' label-prefix character.) Your screen should look like Figure 3.12.

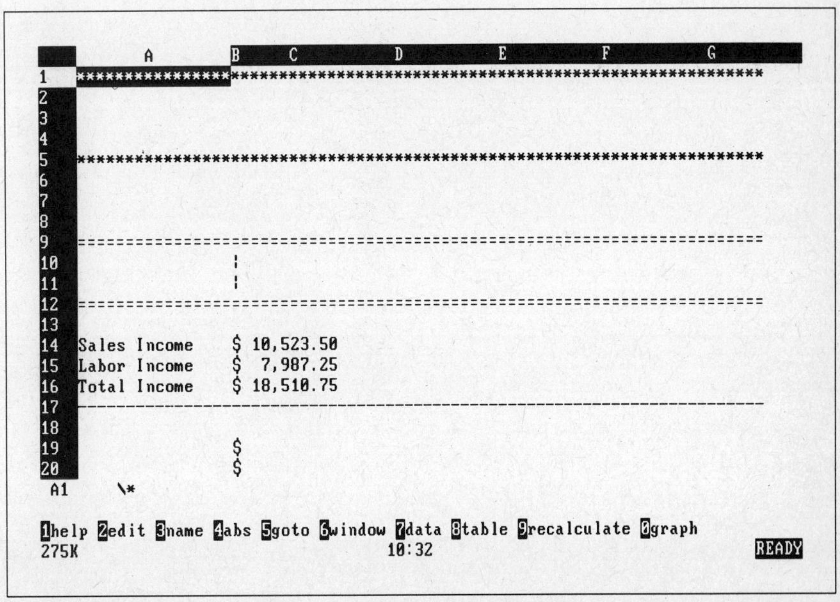

Figure 3.12 Entering Dividing Lines

Step 4: Enter Titles, Headings, and Labels

Now that the dividing lines are done, you're ready to enter the titles, column headings, and row labels that will identify the contents of the worksheet. Typing these labels is easy, although you usually have to experiment a little to get things lined up just right. Fortunately for you, we've already done this alignment.

Move the cell pointer to C2, press the **Space Bar** seven times, and enter **Kwik Key & Lock**. Now move to cell C3, press the **Space Bar** five times, and enter **1404 Silver Street**. To complete the address, move the cell pointer to C4, press the **Space Bar** three times, and enter **Urbana, Illinois 61801**. Move down to cell C7, press the **Space Bar** once, and enter **YEARLY INCOME STATEMENT 1989**.

Now let's enter the column of row labels along the left side of the worksheet. Move to A10 and enter **^Item**. The ^ (caret) is a label-prefix character that tells VP-Planner Plus to center the label that follows within the cell. This feature is rather handy for quickly centering labels within cells without having to count characters and space over.

There is a second way to center labels. Move to cell A13 and type **INCOME**. Call up the Main menu and select the Range command. Press **l** to select the Label option, then press **c** to center a label. Now VP-Planner Plus asks you to specify the range of cells to be altered. In this case, we want the range it suggests, **a13..a13**, so press **Enter**. Note that the word *INCOME* is centered in cell A13, but changes to *^INCOME*.

Enter **EXPENSES** into cell A18 and center the label using either method.

Now move to cell A16, the cell with *Total Income* in it. Examine the completed Kwik Key & Lock income statement in Figure 3.9 and notice how the *Total Income* label is shifted to the right. To do this without having to space over, you could use the right-justification label-prefix character, a " (double quote). You could also use the Range Label command again; this time press **r** for right. Edit this cell to make it look like Figure 3.9. Use what you've learned about label-prefix characters to complete the row labels along the left side as well as the column headings in rows 10 and 11. When you're done, move back to A1. Your screen should look like Figure 3.13.

Figure 3.13 Row Labels and Column Headings for Income Statement

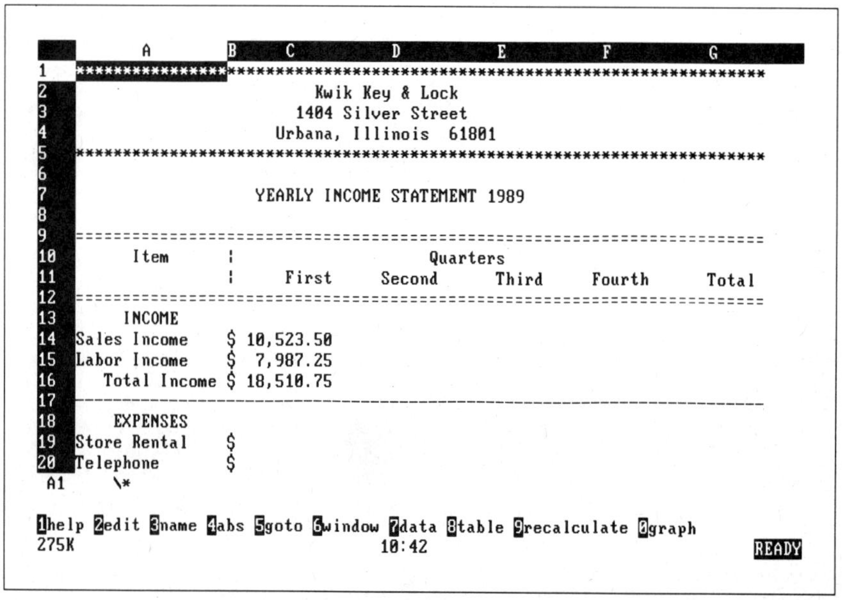

Lesson 7: Completing the Income Worksheet

After you've set up the skeleton of the worksheet, you face the real work: entering the numbers and formulas that give the worksheet meaning. To complete the Kwik Key & Lock income statement, you must type in the income and expense figures and formulate the totals to yield the bottom line net profit for the year.

Step 1: Enter the Numbers

Entering data is perhaps the most tedious part of constructing a worksheet. Although sometimes data can be imported into a worksheet from another worksheet or from the output of some other program, most of the time you must simply type them in yourself. In this case you'll have to enter the raw data—those numbers that aren't calculated from other numbers. Examine the completed Kwik Key & Lock income statement. The raw data consist of all the numbers except those in the column labeled *Total* and those in the rows labeled *Total Income*, *Total Expenses*, *Tot. Deductions*, and *Net Profit*. Go through the worksheet, moving the cell pointer to the appropriate cells and typing the raw data numbers. To save some typing, you can use the Copy command to replicate figures that repeat across several columns, like expenses such as store rental, telephone, utilities, advertising, insurance, tax and licenses, payroll, and depreciation. When you are finished, your screen will look like Figure 3.14.

Figure 3.14 Filling in the Worksheet

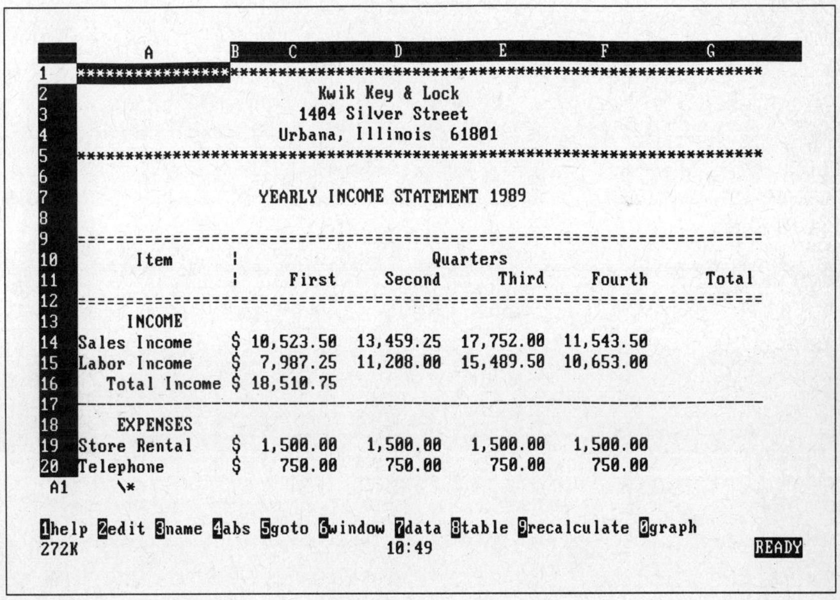

```
          A          B     C          D          E          F          G
1  ***************************************************************************
2                                  Kwik Key & Lock
3                                 1404 Silver Street
4                               Urbana, Illinois  61801
5  ***************************************************************************
6
7                              YEARLY INCOME STATEMENT 1989
8
9  ===========================================================================
10       Item          :                       Quarters
11                     :       First     Second      Third     Fourth      Total
12 ===========================================================================
13       INCOME
14 Sales Income      $ 10,523.50  13,459.25  17,752.00  11,543.50
15 Labor Income      $  7,987.25  11,208.00  15,489.50  10,653.00
16    Total Income   $ 18,510.75
17 ---------------------------------------------------------------------------
18      EXPENSES
19 Store Rental      $  1,500.00   1,500.00   1,500.00   1,500.00
20 Telephone         $    750.00     750.00     750.00     750.00
 A1      \*

1help 2edit 3name 4abs 5goto 6window 7data 8table 9recalculate 0graph
272K                              10:49                                READY
```

Step 2: Enter the Formulas for Total Income

Now that the hard work is out of the way, all that's left to do is fill the empty rows and columns with the appropriate formulas and let VP-Planner Plus compute the totals. You've already entered one of the formulas in cell C16. Instead of typing corresponding formulas in cells D16 through G16, you can use the Copy command to replicate the formula in C16. Move the cell pointer to C16. Type **/c** to select the Copy command, and press **Enter** to copy from cell C16. Now type **d16..g16** as the range to copy to, and press **Enter**. VP-Planner Plus will replicate the formula throughout the row, automatically adjusting the cell references. In other words, the formula *+C14+C15* will become *+D14+D15* when it's copied to cell D16, *+E14+E15* when it's copied to cell E16, and so on. Move the cell pointer through these cells and confirm this by examining the contents of the cells as displayed in the control panel. In the worksheet, you should see the totals displayed in cells D16, E16, and F16. Cell G16 just has a zero in it because the cells' sums are still blank. Your screen should look like Figure 3.15.

Figure 3.15 Entering Formulas for Total Income

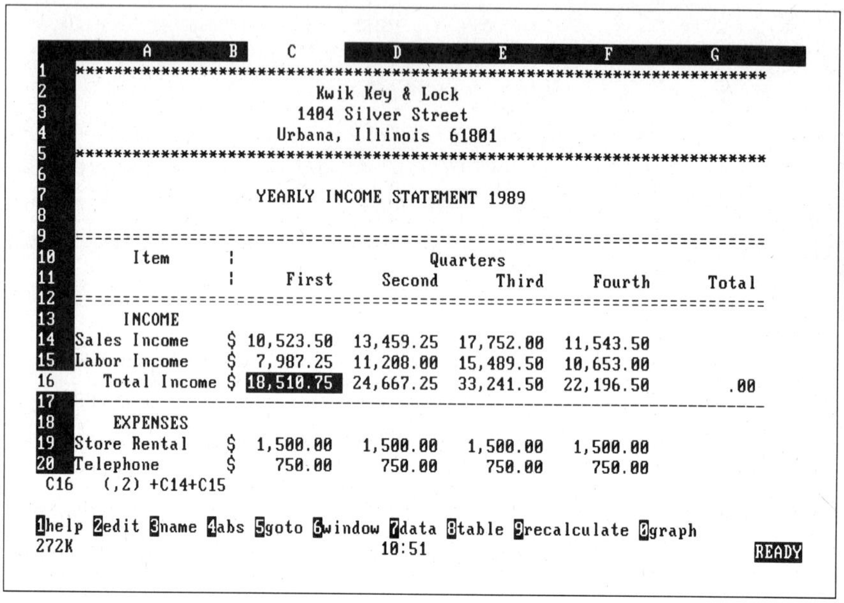

Step 3: Enter the Formulas for Total Expenses

To enter the formula for the first quarter total expenses, move the cell pointer to C33. What you really want here is the sum of cells C19 through C32. Fortunately, VP-Planner Plus provides a handy function that can do that operation for you. A function is sort of a mathematical shortcut that lets you perform common computations with a minimum of typing. VP-Planner Plus has many such functions that can help abbreviate what would otherwise be long and cumbersome formulas. Probably the most frequently used VP-Planner Plus function is @SUM, which adds up the contents of a range of cells. The @ character, which must begin every function name, tells VP-Planner Plus that what follows is the name of a function, not a label. To compute the total expenses for the first quarter, type **@sum(c19..c32)** into cell C33 and press **Enter**. To compute the rest of the total expenses across row 33, use the Copy command to replicate the formula in C33 to cells D33 through G33.

Step 4: Enter the Formulas for Total Deductions

The row labeled *Tot. Deductions* represents the sum of all expenses, depreciation, and bad debts. To compute those figures, move to cell C38, type **@sum(c33..c36)**, and press **Enter**. Then copy that formula to cells D38 through G38. Notice how

VP-Planner Plus ignores labels and blank cells when they are included in a range passed to the @SUM function.

Step 5: Enter the Formulas for Net Profit

The net profit for a given quarter is the total income less the total deductions. Move to cell C40, type **+c16–c38**, and press **Enter**. Now copy that formula to cells D40 through G40.

Step 6: Enter the Formulas for Grand Totals

The only thing left to do to complete the income statement is fill in the formulas to compute the figures for the *Total* column along the right edge. Move to cell G14, type **@sum(c14..f14)**, and press **Enter**. Now copy cell G14 to cells G15, G19 through G32, G35, and G36. If you move the cell pointer back to A1, your screen should look like Figure 3.16. The net profit shown in cell G40 should equal $30,258.38. If your worksheet displays a different number here, go back and check your entries.

Figure 3.16 Completed Income Statement with Data and Totals

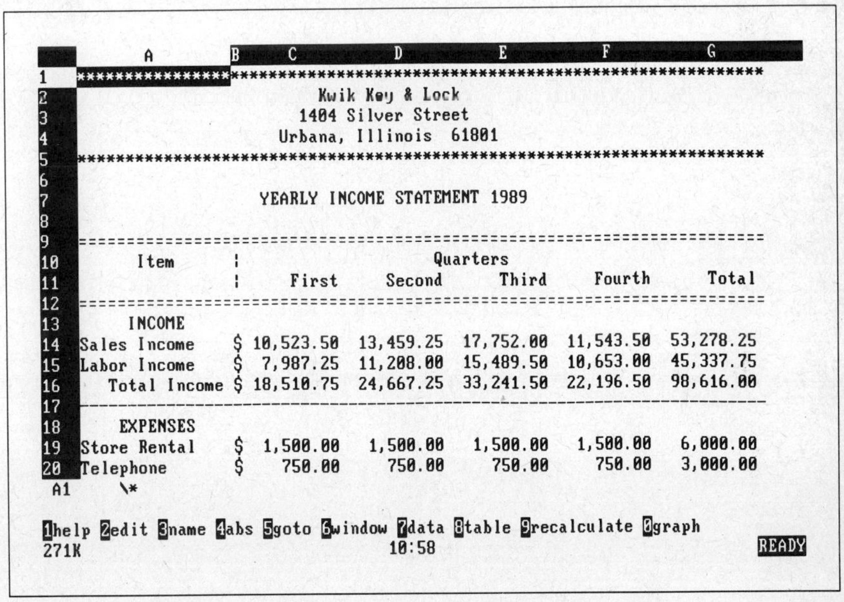

Lesson 8: Saving the Worksheet

Once you've put all that effort into creating a spreadsheet, you're likely to want to store it on disk. There are several reasons for wanting to save a particular worksheet: to print it later, to reference it in the future, to keep it updated, and to use its basic format to build some other worksheet. In addition, if you're entering a long worksheet, it's a good idea to save it to disk periodically as you're building it. Then if you make some drastic error or the power goes out, you won't lose all your work. You'll still be able to retrieve the data you had the last time you saved your worksheet.

Step 1: Select the File Save Command

Most of VP-Planner Plus's operations that deal with disk storage are invoked through the File command. To save a file, you choose the Save option of the File command. Type **/fs** to execute this option from the READY mode. Your screen should look like Figure 3.17, if you are working from a hard disk.

Figure 3.17 Saving the Worksheet

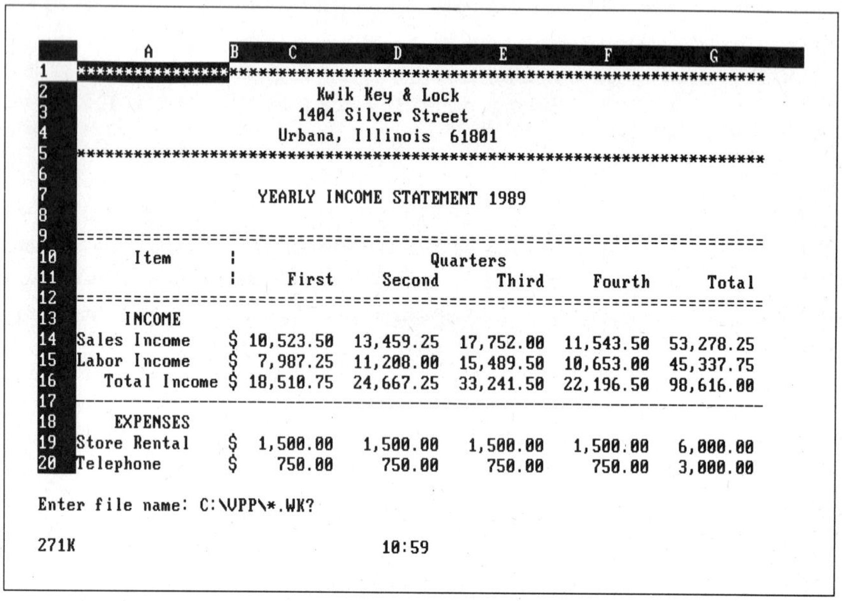

Step 2: Enter a File Name

When you select the Save option, VP-Planner Plus will prompt you with the following for the name of the file in which to store the worksheet:

```
Enter file name: c:\vpp\*.wk?
```

The program will begin this file name with the default directory. If this is where you want to store your file, all you have to do is enter the name you choose. The name you type in will overwrite everything after the second backward slash. If you want to store your worksheet on some other disk drive directory, you can press **Escape** to erase the default directory suggested by VP-Planner Plus. Then you can specify some other disk drive directory and follow it with the name you choose.

Whichever disk drive directory you use, VP-Planner Plus also requires a valid file name. You must give each file a unique name so that you can retrieve the worksheet again. A file name can be up to eight characters long, and can include uppercase and lowercase letters, numbers, and underscores (_). For the Kwik Key & Lock income statement, type **income** and press **Enter**. The VP-Planner Plus program will automatically append the file name extension .WKS to any worksheet file you save. This extension is used so that VP-Planner Plus can tell that a worksheet is stored in that file when you retrieve it later.

Lesson 9: Printing the Worksheet

Most of the time the ultimate purpose of creating a worksheet is to get a copy of the final result on paper. VP-Planner Plus lets you send worksheets to your printer and produce attractive reports with a few simple steps. You can print all or just part of a worksheet from within the VP-Planner Plus program.

Step 1: Turn On Your Printer

Before you can print anything, of course, you must make sure that your printer is turned on and that it's on-line (connected to the computer).

Step 2: Execute the Print Command

To print the worksheet that's currently in memory (the one you're working on), type **/p** to select VP-Planner Plus's Print command. When you do this, VP-Planner Plus will give you a choice of two options: Printer and File. To send your output directly to the printer, you would choose Printer. To create a print file, which you could use in another program (like a word processor) or later print from DOS, you would choose File. For now, type **p** or press **Enter** to send your output directly to the printer. VP-Planner Plus will present you with the screen shown in Figure 3.18.

Figure 3.18 Selecting the Print Range

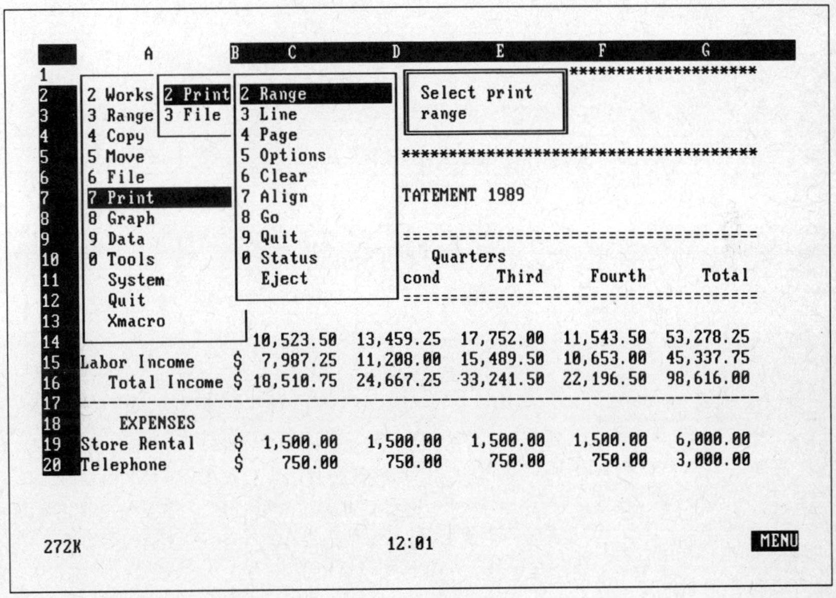

Step 3: Select the Range to Print

Before you can print your worksheet, you must specify the exact range of cells you want VP-Planner Plus to print. By allowing you to specify this range, VP-Planner Plus lets you print all or just part of your worksheet. In this case, we want to print the entire worksheet. Type **r** or press **Enter** to select the Range option. The VP-

Planner Plus program will prompt you to enter a print range. Type **a1..g41** and press **Enter** to specify your entire worksheet.

Step 4: Align the Paper

To guarantee that VP-Planner Plus will print properly on each page of paper, make sure the paper in the printer is lined up at the top of a new page. You can adjust the paper manually or advance it one line at a time by selecting the Line option. When you're all set, select the Align option to tell VP-Planner Plus that the printer is ready to begin printing at the top of a new page.

Like many other VP-Planner Plus operations, a number of default settings are used to control the format of a printed report. Most of the time the format that VP-Planner Plus automatically uses when printing worksheets is good enough. You can, however, select Options to change margins and the page length, establish headers and footers, number pages, and other formatting commands.

Step 5: Select the Go Option

Finally, to actually print the worksheet, type **g** to select the Go option. When VP-Planner Plus is done printing, type **q** for Quit or press **Escape** three times to return to READY mode. Your printout should look like the finished Kwik Key & Lock income statement that appears in Figure 3.9. (NOTE: VP-Planner Plus does not automatically advance the paper to the top of the next page when it is finished printing a worksheet.)

Lesson 10: Retrieving an Existing Worksheet

Now that you've saved and printed your completed worksheet, let's say that you're done for the day. Typically, you'd exit VP-Planner Plus with the Quit command, return to DOS, and continue using your computer for other work or simply shut it off. Now pretend it's sometime later—maybe an hour, maybe a week. You want to use VP-Planner Plus again to view your Kwik Key & Lock income statement and perhaps add or change some data.

Step 1: Invoke VP-Planner Plus

To enact the preceding scenario, first type **/qy** to exit VP-Planner Plus and return to DOS. Now pretend it's sometime later and you want to use VP-Planner Plus again to view the Kwik Key & Lock worksheet. The first step, of course, is to run the VP-Planner Plus program. Type **vpp** and press **Enter**.

Step 2: Execute the File Retrieve Command

To load a previously stored worksheet from disk storage into primary memory, type **/fr** to execute the File Retrieve command. VP-Planner Plus will look in the startup directory for those files that end with the extensions .WKS and .WK1 and display their names in the control panel (see Figure 3.19).

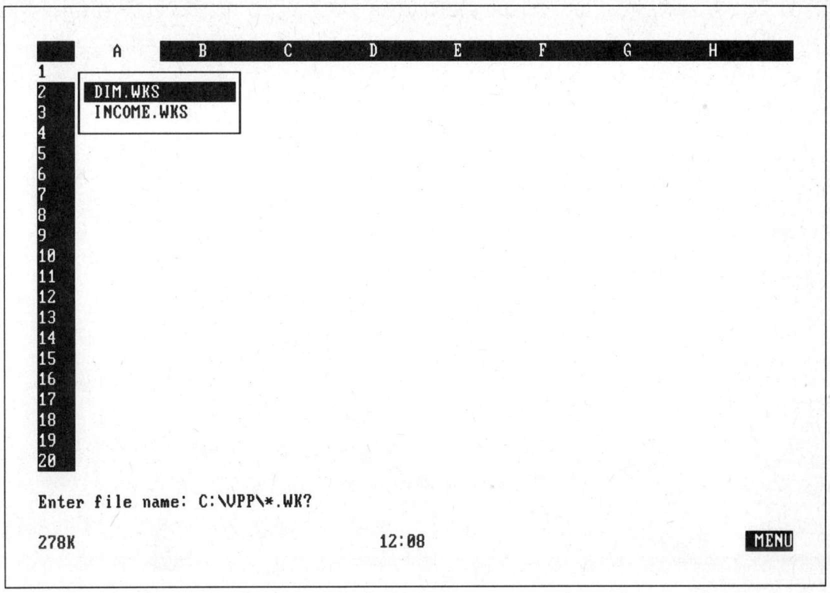

Figure 3.19 Retrieving the Income Statement File

Step 3: Select the Worksheet File

If the worksheet file you want to retrieve is in the list of files that VP-Planner Plus finds in your default directory, all you have to do is use the Up or Down Arrow key to highlight its name and press Enter. For now, highlight *INCOME.WKS* and press **Enter**. If the worksheet you want is stored in some other disk drive directory, press **Escape** and enter the file name preceded by the path. The VP-Planner Plus program will read the file from disk storage, load it into primary memory, and display it on your screen.

Lesson 11: Modifying an Existing Worksheet

Now that you know the basics of creating, saving, printing, and retrieving worksheets, you can expand your knowledge to include other VP-Planner Plus commands for manipulating data. Since you've already had practice retyping and editing labels, numbers, and formulas stored in cells, this lesson will focus on commands that mainly help you rearrange worksheets.

Step 1: Move Data within a Worksheet

You've already learned how to use the Copy command to replicate data from one part of a worksheet to another. A related VP-Planner Plus command is Move, which transfers a range of cell entries from one part of a worksheet to another. It's like the Copy command, except that cells are erased when data are moved from them. Like the Copy command, Move automatically adjusts all cell addresses in formulas that are transferred.

To see how Move works, let's say that you wanted the row of labels along the left side of the worksheet moved to the right side. All you have to do is move column A to column H. Type **/m** to execute the Move command. VP-Planner Plus will ask for the range to be moved. Type **a1..a41** and press **Enter**. Then VP-Planner Plus will ask for the destination. Type **h1..h41** and press **Enter**. All the cells in column A will clear. Use the **Right Arrow** key to move the cell pointer to H1. Figure 3.20 shows what you should see on your screen.

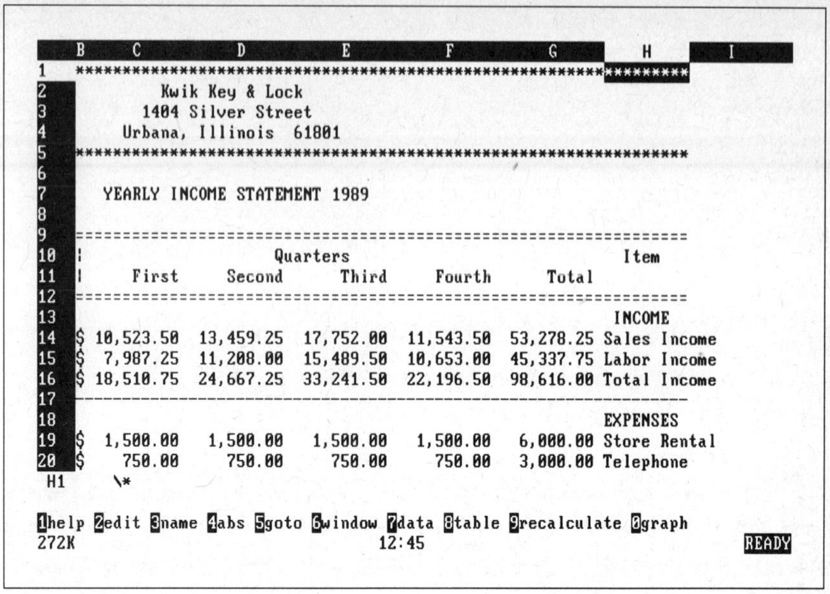

Figure 3.20 Labels Shifted with Move Command

Step 2: Insert Blank Rows or Columns

Quite often you find that you have to add to a worksheet data that you didn't originally plan to add. In the Kwik Key & Lock income statement, for example, you might discover that you need a new row for some expense you didn't foresee. Let's say that Kwik Key & Lock took out a loan and that they now had to pay back that loan in quarterly installments. Move the cell pointer to C32. Type /wir to execute the Worksheet Insert Row command. The VP-Planner Plus program will ask you for the row insert range, and suggest the address of the current cell. Press **Enter** to insert a blank row in that position. Existing rows move down to make room for the new blank row 32. VP-Planner Plus automatically adjusts any cell addresses in formulas so that they refer to the same data. Now enter **500** in cells C32, D32, E32, and F32; the **$** into cell B32 (don't forget to use the label-prefix character '); **@sum(c32..f32)** into cell G32; and **Loan Payment** into cell H32. Note how VP-Planner Plus automatically recalculates the Total Expenses figures in row 34, as well as all other dependent figures in the whole worksheet, to include the new entries (see Figure 3.21). Inserting blank columns works the same way, except that you type **/wic** to execute Worksheet Insert Column.

Step 3: Erase Data

Just as you can insert data into a worksheet, you can use VP-Planner Plus to delete data. In fact, there are three different ways you can erase data from a worksheet. The first method lets you erase the contents of a specific range of cells. For example, to erase the four quarterly loan payments you just entered, move the cell pointer to C32. Type **/re** to execute the Range Erase command. The VP-Planner Plus program will prompt you to enter the range to erase. Type **c32..f32** or press the **Right Arrow** key three times to select the four 500.00 values, and press **Enter**. Those cells will be erased, and all dependent figures will be recalculated as if zeros were in the erased cells.

Figure 3.21 Row Inserted in the Worksheet

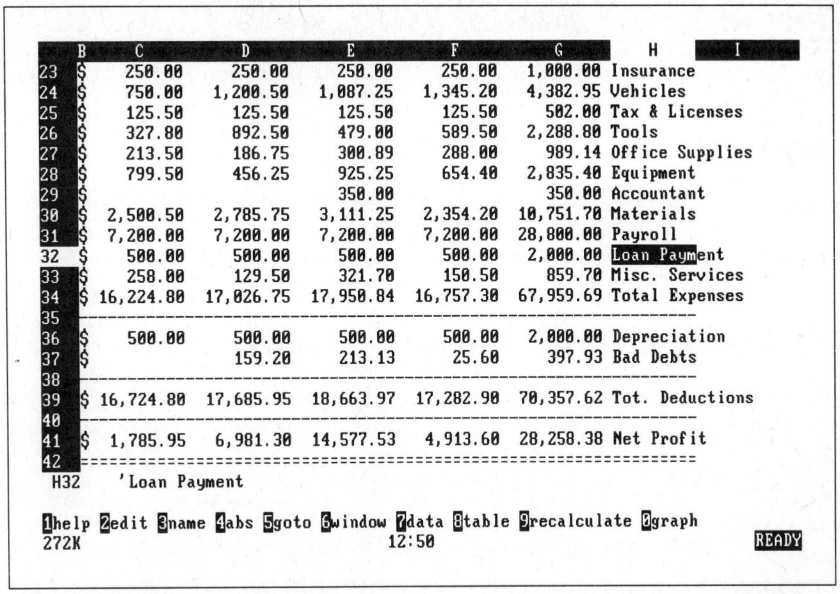

The second method of erasing data allows you to delete entire rows or columns of cells. To try it out, type **/wdr** to execute the Worksheet Delete Row command. VP-Planner Plus will ask you for the range of rows to delete and will suggest the current row. Press **Enter**; the current row 32 will be completely removed and the rows below will move up to close the gap. This command is the opposite of the Worksheet Insert command and can also be used to delete entire columns.

The final method of erasing data in a worksheet is the most drastic. It allows you to erase the entire contents of the current worksheet at once. Type **/we** to execute the Worksheet Erase command. VP-Planner Plus will give you a chance to change your mind. If you really do want to erase everything, type **y** for yes; otherwise type **n** for no. Go ahead and erase the worksheet. The VP-Planner Plus program will erase every cell to give you a blank worksheet, and it will reset default values for column widths and number formats. Note that this command erases only the worksheet that's currently in memory. You won't lose what you have stored on disk unless you do a File Save to replace INCOME.WKS.

Step 4: Save Part of a Worksheet

Sometimes you'd like to split an existing worksheet into smaller parts, or use one portion of a worksheet in another worksheet. VP-Planner Plus lets you accomplish these tasks very easily through the use of the File Xtract command. This command saves a specified range of cells from the current worksheet in a separate worksheet file. It does this without erasing any data in the current worksheet

Since you erased your income statement worksheet in the last step, load it again into memory with the File Retrieve command. Let's try saving just the INCOME portion of it in another worksheet file. To do this, first move the cell pointer to A11. Type **/fx** to execute the File Xtract command and VP-Planner Plus will present you with four choices. We are only concerned with the Formulas and Values options. To save the formulas in the current worksheet in the extract file, you'd select Formulas. If you want to save just numbers, labels, and the values resulting from formulas, but not the formulas themselves, you would choose Values. For this example, type **v** to select Values. VP-Planner Plus will then ask you for the name of the file in which to save the range you're extracting. Type **income2** and press **Enter**. Next you're asked to enter the range of cells you want to extract. Type **a11..g16** or use the **Arrow** keys to highlight that range and press **Enter**. The disk drive access light will go on as VP-Planner Plus creates the file INCOME2.WKS and you'll be returned to READY mode when it's done.

To see what you've created, type /fr to execute the File Retrieve command and select the file INCOME2.WKS. The previous worksheet will be cleared from your screen, and you will see displayed a screen that looks like Figure 3.22.

Figure 3.22 INCOME2.WKS File Retrieved

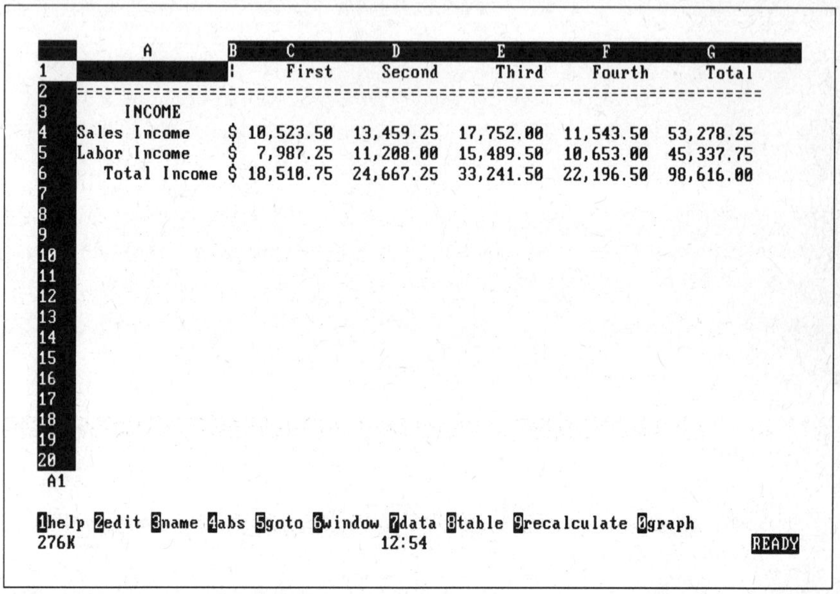

	A	B	C	D	E	F	G
1			First	Second	Third	Fourth	Total
2	========		========	========	========	========	========
3	INCOME						
4	Sales Income	$	10,523.50	13,459.25	17,752.00	11,543.50	53,278.25
5	Labor Income	$	7,987.25	11,208.00	15,489.50	10,653.00	45,337.75
6	Total Income	$	18,510.75	24,667.25	33,241.50	22,196.50	98,616.00

Move the cell pointer around the worksheet and watch the entries as they're presented in the control panel. Notice that now there are only labels and numbers in the cells. No formulas were saved; what remains are only the values that the formulas produced.

Step 5: Retrieve Part of a Worksheet

If you wanted to take the worksheet portion you've just extracted and include it in another worksheet, you would use VP-Planner Plus's File Combine command. This very useful command incorporates all or part of a worksheet file into the current worksheet at the location of the cell pointer. It uses the current cell as the upper-left corner of the incoming data. You have three options when using the File Combine command:

Copy Replace the corresponding entries in the current worksheet with the incoming values

Add Add incoming values to the corresponding entries in the current worksheet

Subtract Subtract incoming values from the corresponding entries in the current worksheet

To try out this command, move the cell pointer to A8. Type /**fcc** for File Combine Copy. VP-Planner Plus will present you with three choices: Entire File, Named Range, and Worksheet. If you choose the first option, the whole incoming worksheet will be incorporated into the current worksheet but the current worksheet's range names and column widths are not affected. If you choose the second option, you'll be allowed to enter a range of cells from the incoming worksheet; only those will be included in the current worksheet. If you choose the third option, the entire worksheet including range names and column widths is incorporated into the current worksheet. For now, just type **e** or press **Enter** to choose the Entire-File option. The VP-Planner Plus program will then ask you for the name of the worksheet file you want to combine—in other words, the file you want to include into the current worksheet. Let's just include again the INCOME portion that you previously saved in file INCOME2.WKS. Use the **Down Arrow** key to highlight INCOME2.WKS and press **Enter**. VP-Planner Plus will copy the contents of that file into the current worksheet. You'll wind up with two copies of the INCOME portion of the original Kwik Key & Lock income statement—one below the other. Leaving the cell pointer in the same place, now try the Add option of the File Combine command with the same INCOME2.WKS file. Notice how the values all double as they are added to themselves (see Figure 3.23). Now try the Subtract option and see how the numbers divide in half, back to the way they were before. If you use the Add or Subtract option on a blank section of the screen, only the numbers will appear, not the labels.

Figure 3.23 Combining Entries in the Worksheet

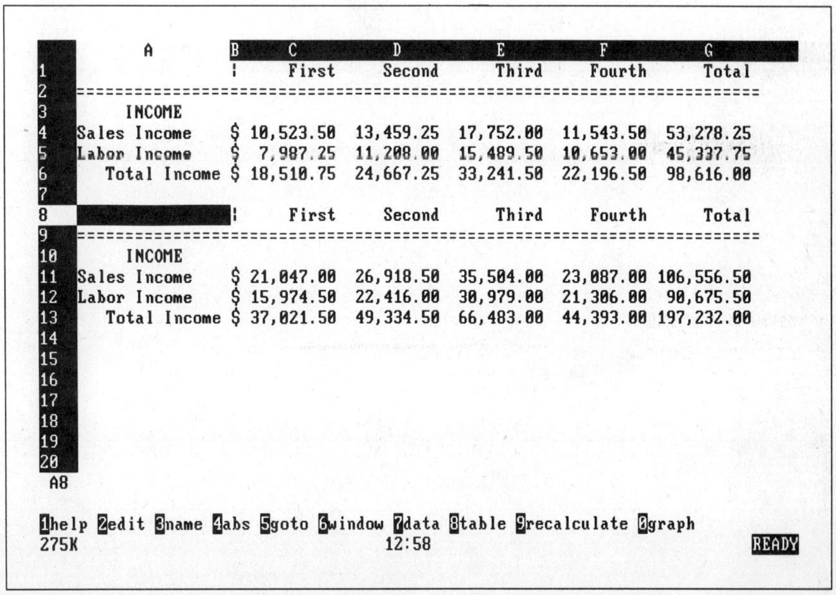

Lesson 12: Learning More About Formulas

As we've said before, a formula is a computational expression that can be stored in a cell. You've used a few formulas in the Kwik Key & Lock income statement to add, subtract, and sum numeric values stored in cells. In fact, formulas can be used to do much more. Let's spend some time covering VP-Planner Plus formulas in a bit more detail.

Step 1: Set Up an Example Worksheet

To illustrate some of the properties of formulas, we're going to have you clear the Kwik Key & Lock income statement and set up a much simpler worksheet. It will be easier to understand what's going on if you have just a few cells filled. Type **/wey** to erase the worksheet currently on your screen. Now enter the labels **One**, **Two**, and **Three** into cells A1, A2, and A3, respectively. Enter the values **100**, **200**, and **300** into cells B1, B2, and B3, respectively. You now have the very simple worksheet shown in Figure 3.24.

Figure 3.24 A Simple Worksheet

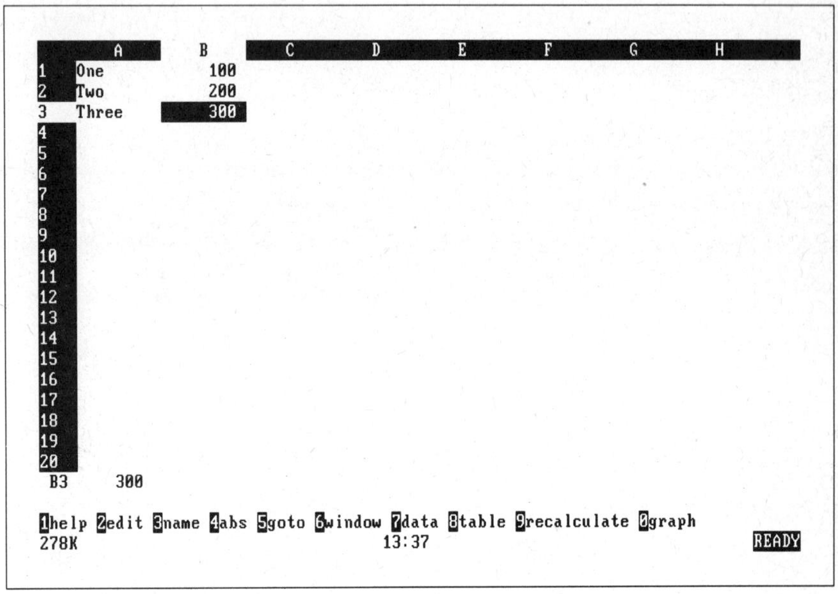

Step 2: Try Three Types of Formulas

VP-Planner Plus allows you to use three basic types of formulas: arithmetic, text, and logical. Arithmetic formulas are mathematical expressions that calculate with numeric values using arithmetic operations such as addition, subtraction, multiplication, division, and exponentiation. Text formulas manipulate labels using the text combination operator, the ampersand (&) character. Finally, logical formulas compare values in two or more cells using logical operations such as greater than, less than, equal to, AND, NOT, and OR. Let's try out some examples to make these formula types more clear.

All the formulas you've entered so far in this chapter have been arithmetic formulas. Just to try another, move the cell pointer to B4, type **+b1+b2+b3**, and press **Enter**. You should see *600* in cell B4.

Although text formulas are used less frequently than either arithmetic or logical formulas, they can be handy in certain situations. The only text formula operator is &, which lets you combine labels to make other labels. For example, move the cell pointer to C1. Type **+a1&" Hundred"** and press **Enter**. VP-Planner Plus takes the *One* in cell A1 and combines it with " *Hundred*" to produce *One Hundred* in cell C1.

Logical formulas are used to compare values; they produce either TRUE (symbolized by a value of 1) or FALSE (symbolized by a value of 0) as the final result of their comparisons. For example, let's say that you wanted to see if the value in cell B3 is greater than the value in cell B1. Move the cell pointer to C2, type **+b3>b1**, and press **Enter**. Since 300 is in B3 and only 100 is in B1, the result of the logical formula you just entered is 1 for TRUE (see Figure 3.25). Although this concept may not seem particularly useful right now, you'll see later how comparisons such as these can be combined with logical functions. Such expressions can be used to perform different operations contingent on the values stored in specific cells. This feature gives you the ability to program VP-Planner Plus in a manner similar to what's done with high level programming languages such as BASIC, FORTRAN, and Pascal.

Figure 3.25 A Logical Formula Returning a 1 Meaning True

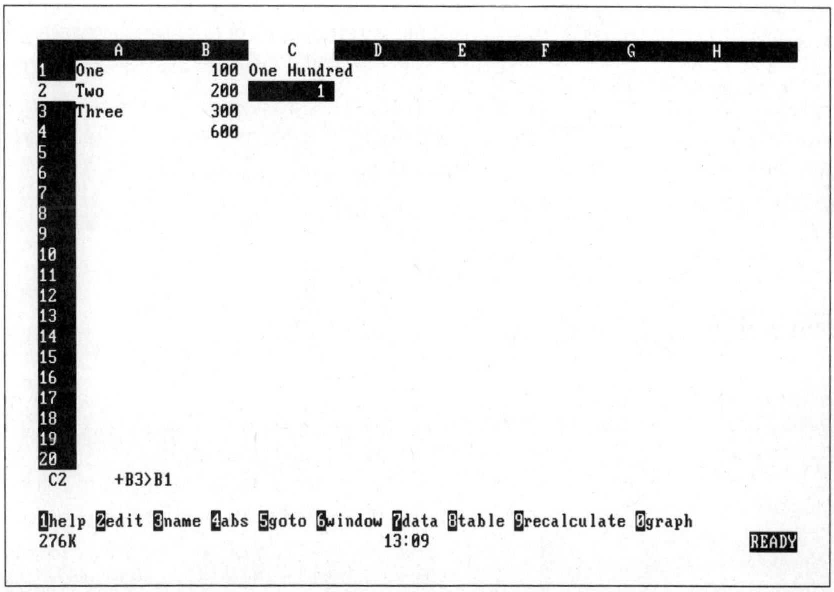

Step 3: Understand What Can Be Included in a Formula

By now you're probably beginning to see just how powerful formulas can be. They give spreadsheet programs such as VP-Planner Plus the flexibility to be applied to so many different kinds of tasks. At this point it's a good idea to summarize the expressions that can be included in formulas. As you read each one, examine or try out the example given with it. These examples will help clarify the concept of a formula even better. VP-Planner Plus allows the following types of symbols and expressions in formulas:

- Operators that symbolize calculation
  (+ – * / = < > &)
- Numbers
  (100+200+300)
- Text strings enclosed in double quotes
  (+"One "&" Hundred")
- Cell addresses
  (+B1+B2+B3)
- Ranges (only used in functions)
  (B1..B3)

- Functions
  (@SUM(B1..B3))
- Combinations of the preceding symbols and expressions
  ((100+200+300+@SUM(B1..B3))>600)

Step 4: Understand the Order of Operations

As you've seen, VP-Planner Plus has several computational operators that can be used in formulas. Like the operators used in mathematics, each one has a precedence associated with it. In other words, when there's more than one type of operator in an expression, there's a specified order in which operations will proceed. For example, move the cell pointer to B5 and enter this expression: **+b1+b2/b3**. If you expect the 100 in B1 to be added to the 200 in B2 and then that result divided by the 300 in B3 to yield 1, you're in for a surprise. The /, which stands for division, is performed before the addition because division has a higher precedence. It's important to understand the precedence order of operators so that you can get your expressions to compute what you want them to. In general, operations of equal precedence are performed from left to right. But some operations have a higher precedence than others. For example, multiplication and division are performed before addition and subtraction; that's why +B1+B2/B3 = 100.6667 instead of 1. Just as you learned in grammar school, however, order of precedence can be altered by using parentheses. For example, if you now enter **(b1+b2)/b3** into cell B5, you'll see that 1 is the result. The parentheses told VP-Planner Plus to do the addition first. When in doubt about the order of operations, use parentheses to force the order you want.

See the table below for a summary of the VP-Planner Plus operators along with their precedence numbers. These numbers represent the precedence in which VP-Planner Plus performs the operations when they're included in a formula without parentheses. Operators with a higher precedence number are performed before those with a lower one. Operators with the same precedence number are executed sequentially from left to right.

Operator	Precedence Number	Operation
^	7	Exponentiation (e.g., 2^3=8)
–	6	Negative (unary minus)
*	5	Multiplication
/	5	Division
+	4	Addition
–	4	Subtraction
=	3	Logical equal
<>	3	Logical not equal
<	3	Logical less than
>	3	Logical greater than
<=	3	Logical less than or equal
>=	3	Logical greater than or equal
#NOT#	2	Logical negation
#AND#	1	Logical conjunction
#OR#	1	Logical disjunction
&	1	String combination

Lesson 13: Learning More About Functions

You've learned that VP-Planner Plus functions are built-in shortcuts that let you perform common operations with a minimum of typing. Like most high-level programming languages, VP-Planner Plus provides a set of functions so that users don't have to construct their own every time they want to do a frequently performed operation. Because they provide convenience and accuracy, built-in functions can greatly facilitate the use of formulas in a worksheet. They include many operations users may have no idea how to do on their own. For example, do you remember how to compute a square root? Even if you do, do you know how to compute it with VP-Planner Plus? Fortunately, there's no need to figure out a computation method because VP-Planner Plus has @SQRT, which will compute a square root for you.

Functions also include operations that may be difficult or even impossible to do in any other way. For example, if you had to sum the values in 1000 cells, you couldn't do it by simply adding the individual cells. Even if you wanted to enter all 1,000 cell addresses and plus signs, VP-Planner Plus wouldn't let you because the maximum number of characters you can enter into a cell is 240. By using @SUM, you can sum 1,000 cells as easily as 3 cells. Obviously, VP-Planner Plus functions can greatly increase the power and improve the accuracy of your formulas.

VP-Planner Plus has more than 100 built-in functions. We cannot, of course, thoroughly cover every one in this lesson. So, we've chosen a few of the most frequently used VP-Planner Plus functions to describe briefly in the following steps. Each step will introduce, explain, and let you try out several important VP-Planner Plus functions.

Step 1: Explore the Mathematical Functions

Mathematical functions compute numeric values given one or more other values. Here are a few of the most frequently used mathematical functions:

@ABS Computes the absolute value of a number or formula result. In other words, it converts a negative value to a positive value. For example, enter this expression into any cell: **@abs(−25)**. Your result should be 25.

@INT Converts a number or formula result to an integer by truncating any fractional part. For example, try entering **@int(2.667)** into any cell. The result should be 2.

@LOG Computes the base 10 logarithm of a number or formula result. For example, try **@log(6.54)**. The result should be 0.8155777.

@MOD Returns the remainder (modulus) from a division operation. For example, enter **@mod(7,3)** into any cell. The result should be 1, the remainder when you divide 7 by 3.

@PI Doesn't really compute anything; it just returns the trigonometric constant π (pi), accurate to fifteen decimal places. Enter **@pi** into any cell. If that cell's width is nine columns, you should get 3.141593.

@RAND Returns a random number between 0 and 1. For example, enter **@rand** into any cell. There's no telling exactly what you might get, but it could be a number such as 0.4075167. Random number generating functions like this are commonly used in statistical and game applications.

@ROUND Rounds a number or formula result to a specified number of decimal places. For example, enter **@round(2.2468,3)** into any cell. VP-Planner Plus will round the 2.2468 to three decimal places and display the result as 2.247.

@SIN Computes the sine of a number or formula result assumed to be expressed in radians. For example, enter **@sin(@pi/2)** into any cell. If you remember your trigonometry, you won't be surprised to see that the result is 1. Notice how functions are combined in this formula example. VP-Planner Plus also includes several other trigonometric functions: @COS (cosine), @TAN (tangent), @ASIN (arc sine), @ACOS (arc cosine), @ATAN (2 quadrant arc tangent), and @ATAN2 (4 quadrant arc tangent).

@SQRT Computes the square root of a number or formula result. Enter **@sqrt(9)** into any cell, and you'll see that the result is 3.

Step 2: Explore the Statistical Functions

Statistical functions perform calculations on lists of values. These lists may be single values, ranges, or combinations of both. Some of the most commonly used VP-Planner Plus statistical functions are:

@AVG Computes the average (or mean) of a list of cells. For example, if you still have 100, 200, and 300 in cells B1 through B3, then enter **@avg(b1..b3)** into any empty cell. The result should be (100+200+300)/3 or 200.

@COUNT Computes the number of nonempty cells in a list of cells. For example, if you still have numbers in cells B1 through B3, then enter **@count(b1..b3)**. Because there are values in every cell in B1..B3, the result should be 3.

@MAX and **@MIN** Return the maximum and minimum value in a list of cells. For example, assuming you still haven't changed B1..B3, try entering **@max(b1..b3)**. The result will be 300. Now try **@min(b1..b3)** to get 100.

@SUM Computes the sum of the values in a list of cells. Actually this function should be an old friend by now. To show that a list can be more than just a range, put **100** in cell C5, move the cell pointer to C6, and try this formula: **@sum(c5,b1..b3,200)**. The result displayed in cell C6 should be 900.

Step 3: Explore the Financial Functions

Since spreadsheets are most often used in the business world, it's not surprising that the VP-Planner Plus includes a rich set of financial functions. These functions are used for calculations concerning loans, annuities, and cash flows that occur over a term (period of time). A few of the useful financial functions are:

@PMT Computes the payment on a loan per payment period for a given principal amount, interest rate, and number of periods. For example, enter **@pmt(4500,0.01,24)** into any cell. This could represent the monthly payment on a new car loan of $4500 (the principal), at 1% per month (12% annual) interest rate, for twenty-four monthly payment periods. If you round it to the nearest cent, the result is a monthly payment of $211.83.

@PV Computes the present value of an investment, given the payment amount, interest rate, and number of periods. Let's say that you just won $2 million in the state lottery. You're given the option of receiving twenty annual payments of $100,000 ($2 million) or an immediate single lump sum payment of $800,000. Assuming you would invest the annual $100,000 payments at 12% interest rate, compounded annually, which would be the better deal? Enter this formula into any cell: **@pv(100000,12%,20)**. The result shows that the $2 million paid over twenty years is worth $746,944.40 in present dollars. Take the $800,000.

@FV Computes the future value of an investment, based on a given payment, interest rate, and term. Let's say that you plan to deposit $1,000 a year into your bank account for the next twenty-five years. Your bank is paying 7% interest, compounded annually and paid on the last day of each year. Assuming you deposit your $1,000 on the last day of each year, how much will your investment be worth in twenty-five years? Enter **@fv(1000,7%,25)** into any cell. Your nest egg will be $63,249.04 at the end of twenty-five years.

@TERM Computes the number of payment periods in the term of an ordinary annuity (an investment yielding fixed yearly payments) necessary to accumulate a given future value. Given the scenario we just presented in the @FV example, how long will it take you to accumulate $100,000? Enter **@term(1000,7%,100000)** into any cell. The result is 30.73431, meaning that it will take about thirty-one years.

Step 4: Explore the Date and Time Functions

VP-Planner Plus converts dates and times into serial numbers, which can be used in calculations. Each day between January 1, 1801 and December 31, 2099 is assigned a sequential date number. January 1, 1801 is converted to –36157; January 2, 1801 is converted to –36156; and so on up until December 31, 2099, which is converted to 73050. The total time in each day is represented by the number 1. The time number for midnight is 0.0; for noon, it's 0.5; and just before midnight, it's 0.99999. Although this might seem like a strange way of keeping time, VP-Planner Plus allows you to convert date and time numbers back to the format you're used to seeing. The date and time functions include:

@DATE Given a year, month, and day, this function returns the corresponding VP-Planner Plus date number. For example, move the cell pointer to cell E1 and enter: **@date(89,12,31)**. The result for December 31, 1989 is 32873. This value can now be used in calculations or logical expressions.

@DAY, @MONTH, and @YEAR Given a date number, these three functions return the numbers for day, month, and year we normally use. For example, move the cell pointer to some empty cell and enter **@day(e1)**. The result is 31, just as you'd expect. Now try @MONTH and @YEAR too.

@TIME Given an hour (0–23), minute (0–59), and second (0–59), this function returns the corresponding VP-Planner Plus time number. For example, move to cell F1 and enter: **@time(14,10,20)**. VP-Planner Plus will return 0.5905093 to represent 14:10:20 (20 seconds after 2:10 P.M., in military format).

@HOUR, @MINUTE, and @SECOND Given a time number, these three functions return the numbers for hour, minute, and second we normally use. For example, move the cell pointer to an empty cell and enter: **@hour(f1)**. VP-Planner Plus will return 14. Now try @MINUTE and @SECOND too.

@NOW Returns the full serial number for the current date and time based on what you entered when you booted up DOS. Move to cell G1 and enter **@now**. VP-Planner Plus will display some number like 3256.47. The actual number you see is dependent upon the date and time entered when you booted DOS. To see how you can use @NOW, try entering these expressions:

@year(@now)	**@hour(@now)**
@month(@now)	**@minute(@now)**
@day(@now)	**@second(@now)**

Step 5: Explore the Logical Functions

Logical functions return values that are contingent on the results of conditional expressions. They essentially allow you to compare values in cells and perform different actions based on the results of those comparisons. Some of the logical functions include:

@ISNUMBER and @ISSTRING Allow you to determine whether the contents of a cell is a number or string (label). If the cell contains a formula, the value resulting from that formula will be examined. For example, enter **@isnumber(e1)** into some empty cell. If you still have the date number in E1, the result will be 1 for TRUE. Now try **@isstring** on that same cell. This time, your result should be 0 for FALSE.

@IF Evaluates a given logical expression as TRUE or FALSE, and returns the first value given if TRUE, or the second value given if FALSE. For example, move the cell pointer to some empty cell. Enter this formula: **@if(b1>100,"Big", "Small")**. This formula says that if the value in cell B1 is greater than 100, then enter *Big* in the current cell; if it's less than or equal to 100, enter *Small* in the current cell. If you still have 100 in B1 you should see *Small* in your current cell.

@CHOOSE Selects a value from a list based on the first item given. For example, move to an empty cell and enter the following : **@choose(b2/100–1,"Small","Medium","Large")**. If you still have 200 in B2, your current cell should say *Medium*. The @CHOOSE function examines the value of the very first item in the parentheses. If the value is 0, it returns the first value in the list that follows; if the value is 1, it returns the second value in the list, and so on. Since B2 contains 200, the result of the expression B2/100–1 is 2 minus 1 (remember the rules of precedence), or l. So, @CHOOSE returns the second value, "Medium," and enters it into the current cell. Use the **F2** key (EDIT mode) to change the B2 in the formula to B3 and see what happens. Now try B1 too.

Lesson 14: Using VP-Planner Plus Macros

In the construction of large worksheets you sometimes find that you are performing the same operations over and over again. This repetition is especially true of worksheets that are used on a regular basis, as is common in business applications. Fortunately, VP-Planner Plus has a very powerful capability that can help with these repetitive operations. The program allows you to enter, name, and replay any collection of keystrokes. These named collections of keystrokes are called **macros**. Because every procedure you perform with VP-Planner Plus consists of a sequence of keystrokes, macros can be used to automate any action you can do manually. Macros are often used for entering the same label many times, performing repetitive procedures that require many keystrokes, automating frequently used commands, and customizing worksheets for those who aren't familiar with VP-Planner Plus. Macros are one of VP-Planner Plus's most advanced features and they can be quite complex. In this lesson, however, our aim is to illustrate the development and use of a very basic macro.

Step 1: Plan the Macro

A macro is a sequence of keystrokes that you can store and give a name to. Once you do this, you can replay the sequence with a single command over and over again. The first step in creating a macro is deciding just what you want it to do. As an example, let's build a macro that automatically enters column headings like some of the ones in the Kwik Key & Lock income statement. Imagine that you are constructing a worksheet that uses the headings *First*, *Second*, *Third*, *Fourth*, and *Total*. Furthermore, these headings are to go into columns C, D, E, F, and G, respectively. The particular worksheet you're designing requires several rows with these same column headings. Instead of manually entering these headings into every row you need them in, you can create a macro and enter them only once. Then every time you need them, you can enter them all with a single command.

To plan the macro, think of how you would do this procedure manually. If it's a very complex macro, you'd probably want to outline the steps on paper or actually try them out once, carefully noting the keystrokes. In this case the steps are pretty straightforward. First, you would move the cell pointer to the beginning (column A) of the current row. Then you would press the Right Arrow key twice to move the cell pointer to column C. Next you would type **First**, press the Right Arrow key, type **Second**, press the Right Arrow key, type **Third**, press the Right Arrow key, type **Fourth**, press the Right Arrow key, and type **Total**. Finally, you'd want to move the cell pointer back to the beginning of the next row.

Step 2: Enter the Macro Definition

Before you can use a macro, you must first define it. This definition tells VP-Planner Plus what keystrokes to execute when you invoke the macro. A macro definition is entered into a worksheet as a series of labels stored in cells. To try this out, clear your current worksheet by typing **/wey**. The first step in entering a macro definition is to move to an unused portion of the worksheet. Macro definitions aren't data or labels that you normally want displayed in your finished worksheet. Usually, they're placed in cells below or to the right of the area the actual worksheet is expected to occupy. For this example, move the cell pointer to B13.

You may type the label entries of a macro definition in any column of cells. Furthermore, you can type more than one macro instruction in any cell, as long as you don't try to enter more than 240 characters in a single cell. Every cell entry in a macro definition must be a label; numbers and formulas will be translated when the macro is invoked. The entries in a macro definition may consist of any character you can type on your keyboard, like A, B, C, 1, 2, 3, +, −, =, @, $, %, and so on. In addition, some other keys that perform actions instead of displaying characters can also be included in macro definitions. These special keys are included in macro definitions by entering a symbol or a name enclosed in braces ({ and }). For example, to include the Right Arrow keystroke in a macro definition, you would enter **{right}**. VP-Planner Plus has names for the following special keys so that they can be included in macro definitions:

Key	Macro Definition
Enter	~ (the tilde character)
Down Arrow	{down}
Up Arrow	{up}
Left Arrow	{left}
Right Arrow	{right}
Home	{home}
End	{end}
Page Up	{pgup}
Page Down	{pgdn}
Ctrl-Right Arrow	{bigright}
Ctrl-Left Arrow	{bigleft}
F2 (EDIT Mode)	{edit}
F5 (go to a cell)	{goto}
Escape	{esc} or {escape}
Backspace	{backspace} or {bs}
Delete	{del} or {delete}

To begin the macro definition, enter **{end}{left}** into cell B13. This first entry will tell VP-Planner Plus to move the cell pointer to the beginning of the current row when the macro is invoked. Keep in mind that you're just defining the macro now. The keystrokes you enter won't be executed until you invoke the macro later. To finish up the macro definition, move to the cell listed in the first column and enter what you see in the second column:

B14 **{right}{right}**
B15 **First{right}**
B16 **Second{right}**
B17 **Third{right}**
B18 **Fourth{right}**
B19 **Total{down}**
B20 **{end}{left}**

Your screen should now look like Figure 3.26.

Step 3: Name the Macro

Every macro must have a name so that you can tell VP-Planner Plus to invoke it. A macro name consists of a backslash (\) followed by a letter from A to Z. For example, let's name your macro \L to remind you that it enters labels. To name the macro, move the cell pointer to B13, the first cell of the macro definition. Type **/rnc** to execute the command Range Name Create. This command lets you give a name to a range of cells so that you can more easily refer to that range later. The command is also used to name macros. VP-Planner Plus will ask you to enter the name. Type **\L** and press **Enter**. The VP-Planner Plus program will then ask for the range to name. If the cell pointer is on the first cell in the macro definition, all

Figure 3.26 Macro To Enter Quarterly Heading Labels

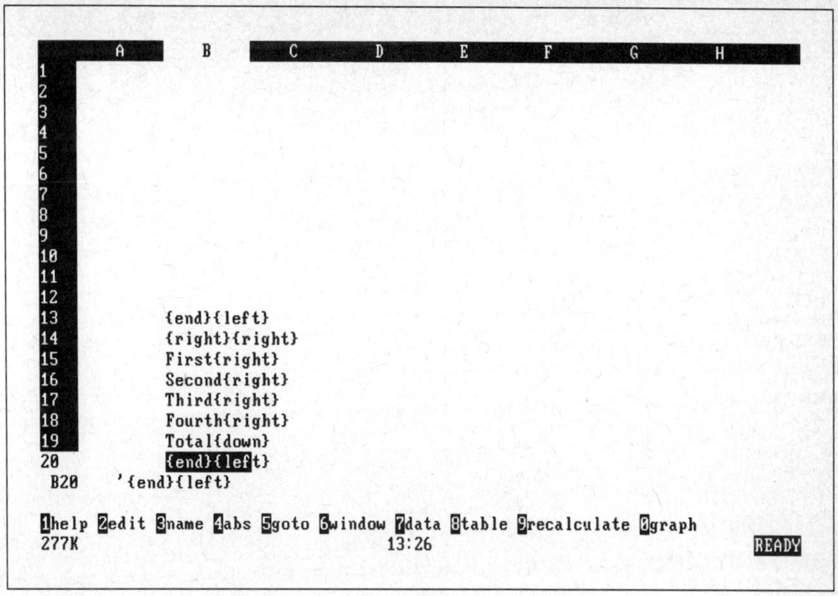

you have to do here is press **Enter**. You will return to READY mode, all set to use your new macro. Before we go on, however, you should perform one more step. A common practice is to document your macro definition so that if you forget its name or what it does you can refer back to it. Move to cell A13, type **'\L**, and press **Enter**. This note in A13 will remind you if you forget that the name of the macro defined next to it in column B is \L. For complex macros, add some description of what the macro does beside it in column A or D. Move to cell D13 and enter **Macro to enter quarterly heading labels**.

Step 4: Invoke the Macro

Now that you've defined and named the macro, you're all ready to actually use it. First, move the cell pointer to the row where you want to enter the labels. How about row 2 for starters? It doesn't matter which column you put the cell pointer in because the macro will automatically move it to the correct column. To invoke a macro, all you have to do is hold down the Alt key and press the letter that names the macro. Press **Alt-L** and watch the screen. Wasn't that fun? Since you can now use Alt-L in any empty row in this worksheet, move to row 5 and try it again. Your screen should look like Figure 3.27.

As you can imagine, VP-Planner Plus macros are an extremely powerful tool. The macro you've just created is a very simple example of what can be done. VP-Planner Plus provides much more advanced macro capabilities that can be used like a high-level programming language by sophisticated users.

Lesson 15: Creating Graphs

If your computer has graphics capabilities, you can use VP-Planner Plus to produce certain types of graphs. This feature can be valuable because graphs let you visualize your data and see them in new ways. People who aren't familiar with spreadsheet formats often find graphs easier to understand. This lesson will show you how to create, save, and print a simple bar graph.

Figure 3.27 Using a VP-Planner Plus Macro

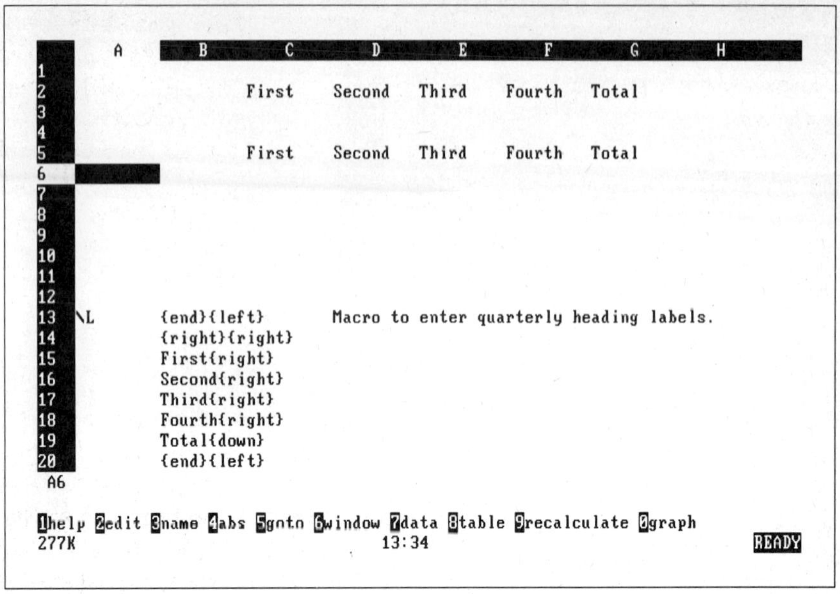

Step 1: Load the Worksheet

Before you can produce a graph, you must have a worksheet from which to extract data. For this example, we'll use the Kwik Key & Lock income statement again. Load the worksheet by typing **/fr** to do a File Retrieve, then enter **income** for the file name.

Step 2: Plan the Graph

For this example, we're going to have you produce a bar graph that displays Kwik Key & Lock's total income for each quarter. So, the horizontal X-axis will have the four quarters, and the vertical Y-axis will show dollars earned. Since VP-Planner Plus also allows you to display titles and axis labels, you should think about how you want to document your graph.

Step 3: Set Up the Graph

To invoke VP-Planner Plus's Graph command, type **/g**. You will see displayed another menu that presents options for setting up and viewing graphs. Select the first option labeled Type to tell VP-Planner Plus what kind of graph you want to produce. You'll be given a choice of five types of graphs: Line, Bar, XY, Stacked-Bar, and Pie. Type **b** to do a bar graph. The next step is to define the X-axis, so type **x** to select the X option of the Graph command menu. VP-Planner Plus will ask for the axis range. Since the X-axis is to show the four quarters of the year, type **c11..f11** and press **Enter**. This action will display the labels *First*, *Second*, *Third*, and *Fourth* as the values along the X-axis. Now type **a** to specify the first (and, in this case, only) range of data for the Y-axis. Type **c16..f16** and press **Enter**. The total income values for each quarter will be displayed along the Y-axis. Now type **o** to select the menu choice labeled Options. Type **t** to specify titles for your graph. Press **Enter** to specify the first title line, type **Kwik Key & Lock**, and press **Enter** again. Type **ts** to specify the second title line, and enter **Quarterly Income for 1989**. Now type **tx** to specify the title for the X-axis.

Type **Quarters** and press **Enter**. Finally, type **ty** to specify the title for the Y-axis and enter **Dollars**.

Step 4: View the Graph

Press **q** once to return from the Options submenu back to the Graph menu. Type **v** for View to have VP-Planner Plus display the graph on your screen. You should see something like Figure 3.28.

When you're done viewing the graph, press any key to return to the Graph command menu.

Figure 3.28 Kwik Key & Lock Quarterly Income Graph

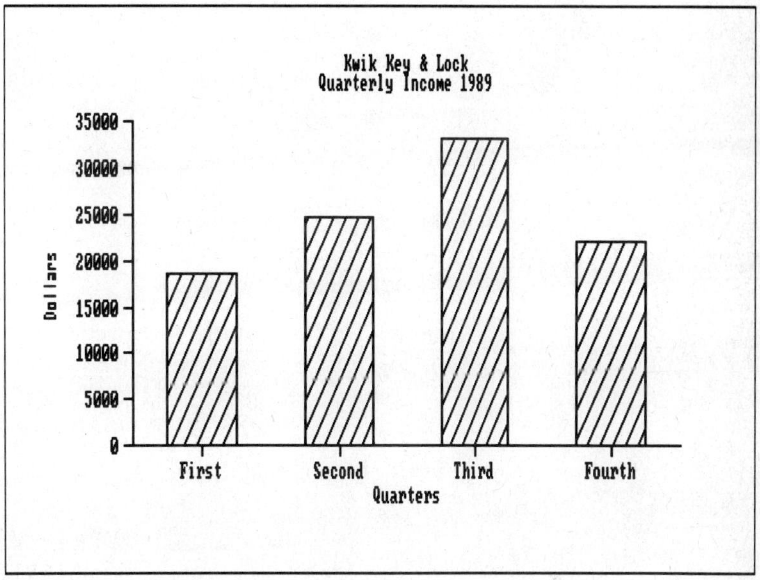

Step 5: Save the Graph

If you ever want to view or print out the graph later, you have to save it. To do this, simply save the worksheet again. Press **/fs** and then press **Enter** to save the worksheet to the disk file INCOME.WKS. The graph settings you have specified will be saved along with the worksheet.

Step 6: Print the Graph

Assuming a printer is connected to your computer, printing the graph is very easy. Press **/gp** to execute the Graph Print command. When the graph has finished printing, press **q** to return from the Graph menu to READY mode.

Conclusion

In this chapter of the *Software Guide*, we've covered the basics of using the VP-Planner Plus program. To be sure, we haven't come close to discussing every capability of this versatile package. We have, however, given you a solid introduction to many of the most frequently used features. Paperback Software has done an excellent job with the documentation for VP-Planner Plus. In addition to the material from Paperback Software, there are several well-written ancillary books on the subject. Finally, we encourage you to experiment with VP-Planner Plus on your own. You'd be surprised how much you can do, armed with what you've learned in this manual, and what you can discover through the help facility and your own curiosity.

Exercises

Multiple Choice

Choose the best selection to completee each statement.

______ 1. To run VP-Planner Plus from a hard disk, which of the following commands do you enter at the DOS prompt?
(a) plus
(b) v-p
(c) vpp
(d) plan

______ 2. A cell is a
(a) worksheet row.
(b) worksheet column.
(c) column-row intersection.
(d) piece of data.

______ 3. A great advantage of electronic spreadsheet programs is that they
(a) contain both columns and rows.
(b) permit scrolling to bring the next portion into view.
(c) let you move to any column or row.
(d) automatically recalculate all formulas.

______ 4. In VP-Planner Plus, how are columns and rows labeled?
(a) Columns are labeled with letters A to IV; rows are labeled with numbers 1 to 9999.
(b) Rows are labeled with letters A to IV; columns are labeled with numbers 1 to 9999.
(c) Columns are labeled with numbers 1 to 256; rows are labeled with letters A to ZZ.
(d) Columns and rows are both labeled with numbers 1 to 256.

______ 5. The three types of data that can be entered into worksheet cells are
(a) headings, text, and labels.
(b) numbers, labels, and formulas.
(c) sums, products, and quotients.
(d) commands, options, and macros.

______ 6. A formula is a(n)
(a) cell name.
(b) instruction that tells VP-Planner Plus to perform some calculations.
(c) sequence of keystrokes that can be named and stored.
(d) list of command options.

______ 7. To use the EDIT mode to modify a cell entry, which key should you press?
(a) Escape
(b) Delete
(c) F1
(d) F2

______ 8. To change from READY mode to MENU mode and have VP-Planner Plus display its Main menu, which key should you press?
(a) /
(b) M
(c) Escape
(d) F1

______ 9. To perform operations on a rectangular block of one or more cells, which of the following Main menu options would you select?
(a) Worksheet
(b) Range
(c) Copy
(d) Move

_____________ 10. The default width of a column of cells in VP-Planner Plus is
(a) seven characters.
(b) eight characters.
(c) nine characters.
(d) ten characters.

_____________ 11. To change the number display format of the entire worksheet, which of the following series of characters would you type?
(a) /WC
(b) /WGF
(c) /RL
(d) /RN

_____________ 12. Which command would you use to replicate numbers, labels, or formulas across several rows or columns?
(a) Worksheet
(b) Range
(c) Copy
(d) Move

_____________ 13. Which of the following file name extensions does VP-Planner Plus use for worksheet files stored on disks?
(a) .WK1
(b) .WKS
(c) .WSF
(d) .WKF

_____________ 14. Which of the following command options would you use to save part of the current worksheet in a disk file?
(a) File Retrieve
(b) File Save
(c) File Combine
(d) File Xtract

_____________ 15. The three types of VP-Planner Plus formulas are
(a) mathematical, statistical, and financial.
(b) arithmetic, text, and logical.
(c) multiplicative, additive, and exponential.
(d) micro, mini, and macro.

_____________ 16. The VP-Planner Plus operator with the highest precedence is
(a) ^ (exponentiation).
(b) * (multiplication).
(c) + (addition).
(d) & (string combination).

_____________ 17. A function is a(n)
(a) cell name.
(b) command option.
(c) mathematical shortcut that returns a value.
(d) arithmetic operator.

_____________ 18. The following are examples of VP-Planner Plus financial functions:
(a) @ABS, @INT, @LOG, @RAND.
(b) @AVG, @COUNT, @MAX, @SUM.
(c) @PMT, @PV, @FV, @TERM.
(d) @DATE, @TIME, @NOW, @IF.

_____________ 19. In VP-Planner Plus, a macro is a
(a) named collection of keystrokes.
(b) function too large to fit in a cell.
(c) mathematical shortcut.
(d) logical formula.

_____________ 20. The following is not one of the Graph Type options:
(a) Line.
(b) Bar.
(c) Stacked-Bar.
(d) Exploded-Wedge.

Fill-in

1. A spreadsheet is a table of _________________ and _________________ of entries.

2. The _________________ is the basic unit of storage in a worksheet—where you enter numbers, labels, and formulas.

3. VP-Planner Plus can address over _________________ million cells.

4. The four lines at the bottom of the VP-Planner Plus worksheet screen are known as the ____________________.

5. To move the cell pointer one cell at a time, you would use one of the ____________________.

6. To move the cell pointer to A1, no matter where it's currently at, you would press the ____________________ key.

7. The three types of data you can enter into worksheet cells are ____________________, ____________________, and ____________________.

8. You can change the contents of the current cell by pressing F2 to invoke VP-Planner Plus's ____________________ mode.

9. Press ____________________ to display VP-Planner Plus's Main menu on your screen.

10. To select an option from a VP-Planner Plus menu, type its first letter, press a function key, or move the highlight block on top of it and press ____________________.

11. A rectangular block of one or more cells is called a ____________________.

12. The ____________________ command is just like the Copy command, except that it erases the contents of the source range.

13. The ____________________ ____________________ command incorporates all or just part of a worksheet file on disk into the current worksheet.

14. Pressing F1 brings up VP-Planner Plus's ____________________ facility.

15. To keep a worksheet for future reference, you would use the File ____________________ command.

16. To load a worksheet file into memory so that you can work on it with VP-Planner Plus, you would use the File ____________________ command.

17. ____________________ formulas are used to compare values; they produce either TRUE (symbolized by a 1) or FALSE (symbolized by a 0) as the final result of their comparisons.

18. Like most high-level programming languages, VP-Planner Plus provides a set of ________________ so that users don't have to construct their formula from scratch every time they want to do a frequently performed operation.

19. To invoke a macro, hold down the ____________________ key and press the letter that names the macro.

20. The ____________________ command lets you send a VP-Planner Plus graph to a printer or plotter.

Short Problems

1. If you aren't already running VP-Planner Plus, invoke the program. If your current worksheet isn't empty, clear it with the Worksheet Erase command. Enter the current year in cell A1, and then use a formula to enter the next year in cell B1. Use the Copy command to enter the next seven years into cells C1 through H1. Use the Range Format command to fix the number of decimal places displayed in cells A3 through H3 to 2. Enter a cost value of 100.00 into cell A3, and by using a formula, enter this cost figure plus 5% into cell B3. Fill cells C3 through H3 by using the Copy command so that each cell is 105% of the cell to the left. Be sure that the only numbers you enter are in cells A1 and A3. All the rest of the cells should contain formulas. This problem shows how you can use a spreadsheet to illustrate things like increasing sales and inflation.

2. In the preceding problem, the 5% increase during each of the eight years was "built-in" to the formula. A variation of this problem would allow the percentage increase to be entered into a cell. The formulas that compute the value beneath each year would then reference this percentage increase instead of using 5%. Alter your worksheet so that it incorporates this change. You can use any empty cell to store the percentage increase value. Try 10%, 15%, and 20% to see how the values change from year to year.

3. Use VP-Planner Plus to formulate and print a simple multiplication table for the numbers 1 through 6. Use these numbers as your row and column headings. Enter the value 1 only. All other headings and the values in the body of the table should be calculated by using formulas and the Copy command.

4. Assume a student takes three exams, which count 20%, 35%, and 45% toward his or her final grade. Construct a VP-Planner Plus worksheet to accept the three exam scores (in any three cells of your choosing) and calculate the final grade.

5. Assume that 10% of the cost of a microcomputer system can be claimed as the salvage value of the system. Of the remaining 90%, 1/7 can be claimed as depreciation in each of the seven years of the life of the system. Create a VP-Planner Plus worksheet that will accept the cost of the system and output the salvage value and the depreciation for each of the seven years of useful life of the system.

6. Use VP-Planner Plus to generate a table of the cube root, square root, square, and cube for each whole number value from 1 to 25. List the number in column A, cube root in column B, square root in column C, square in column D, and cube in column E. Use appropriate labels for column headings, and be sure to use formulas and the Copy command wherever you can.

7. Use VP-Planner Plus to generate the following inventory table. Be sure to have the worksheet calculate the On Hand quantities.

Stock No.	Description	Purchased	Sold	On Hand
10446	Kwik-Zap Eraser	150	20	130
11397	Zippy Pen	40	32	8
24465	Note-O-Pad	450	380	70
46773	Pencilette	25	0	25
58832	Stiky Tapes-It	90	50	40

8. Use VP-Planner Plus to enter the following table. You're going to have to use the Worksheet Column and Range Format commands to set up the worksheet to display such large numbers.

Account Description	Account Balance This Year	Year to Date Last Year
Cash on hand & in banks	344,584,904.00	235,452,143.60
Accounts Receivable	655,473,321.08	527,004,321.97
Inventories	344,733,211.95	130,982,021.80
Land	584,000.00	520,000.00
Buildings	123,894,992.00	864,389.00
Equipment & machinery	1,448,993,406.00	894,600,000.00
Sales	5,945,652,870.00	1,236,772,345.00

9. Use the @RAND function and the Copy command to put random numbers into cells A1 through A10. Notice how a different random number appears in each cell. Now move to B1 and enter a formula containing the @INT function to convert the random number in cell A1 to an integer between 1 and 6 inclusive. Hint: Try @INT(A1*6)+1. Use the Copy command to convert the rest of the numbers in column A to integers in column B. This step will simulate the throwing of a die ten times.

10. Use the @RAND function and the Copy command to simulate 100 coin tosses. Do this by putting a random number into cells A1 through A100. Then convert these numbers to integers between 0 (for heads) and 1 (for tails) in column B. Using the @AVG function, see how close you come to having the fifty heads and fifty tails predicted by the laws of probability.

11. Make up twenty exam grades (between 0 and 100 inclusive), and enter these grades into cells A1 through A20. Use the @MAX and @MIN functions to calculate the range of the grades. Now calculate the average grade.

12. Even though VP-Planner Plus stores dates and times as serial numbers for calculations, you can still get VP-Planner Plus to display them on the screen in conventional formats. Move to cell A1, and execute the Range Format Date command. Choose the DD-MM-YY format. Now widen column A so that it can hold at least twelve characters. Enter **@now** into A1 to display today's date. Move to cell A2, execute the Range Format Date Time command, and select the first format. Enter **@now** into A2 to display the current time.

13. Create a VP-Planner Plus worksheet to calculate the miles per gallon you get on your car (if you don't have a car, pretend you have one and make up values). Inputs will include the odometer reading when the tank is first filled, the odometer reading when the tank is filled the second time, and the number of gallons it took to refill the tank.

14. Using appropriate labels for headings in cells A1 and A2, enter the number of hours a typical student might work per week in cell B1 and the rate of pay per hour in cell B2. Assume that the federal and state income tax rates are 15% and 7%, respectively, and that Social Security (FICA) is another 8%. Create a VP-Planner Plus worksheet to calculate the net income and display it in cell B3.

15. A picture frame shop sells frames at $2.50 per foot. Put an appropriate heading in cell A1 and enter the cost per foot to be charged in cell B1. Cells B2 and B3 should be used to enter the width and height of the picture, and the total cost of the frame should be calculated in B4. Use appropriate headings in the column A cells. Carefully note that one of the inputs is cost/foot and that the other two inputs are the width and height of the frame in inches.

16. Determine the approximate number of hours per week you sleep, eat, watch television, exercise, study, work, and so on (try to come up with ten to twelve activities). Use VP-Planner Plus to prepare a table showing these times and the percentage of the total time in a week each activity consumes.

17. Sewing patterns usually indicate the number of yards of material required for the project. Suppose you like to add 10% to the required material just to be absolutely sure you have enough. Create a VP-Planner Plus worksheet that will accept the number of yards required, as stated on the pattern, along with the cost per yard. Calculate the number of yards to buy and the total price you'll pay (including a 5% state sales tax).

18. Create a VP-Planner Plus worksheet that will accept the price of one share of a stock in cell B1 and the total number of shares purchased in cell B2. The commission charged by the stockbroker is 1% of the total purchase. Calculate the total cost to the purchaser: number of shares times the cost per share, plus the commission.

19. Create a VP-Planner Plus worksheet that will use the date and time functions to calculate the number of hours (rounded to the nearest hour) until your next birthday.

20. It's actually possible to use VP-Planner Plus as a simple word processor! For example, you could set column A to a width of 80 columns. Try typing in a simple memo. Note the lack of word wrap, so you'll have to press the Down Arrow key at the end of each line to enter that line into the worksheet. What are the advantages and disadvantages of using VP-Planner Plus in such a manner?

Long Problems

1. Select a minimum of eight categories of school expenses (tuition, room and board, fees, books, supplies, and so on) and assume realistic values for your freshman year. Enter these labels and values into the first two rows of a VP-Planner Plus worksheet. Using a formula for a 10% increase per year, calculate the value for your first category of your sophomore year. Now copy this formula so that all values for your sophomore year are calculated. Next, use the Copy command to apply the formulas from the sophomore year to your junior and senior years, invoking a 10% rise each year. Do *not* make individual entries in cells except for those assumed values for your freshman year and the formula for the first expense category of your sophomore year. All other cells are to be filled using the Copy command. Next, use the @SUM function to find the total of your freshman year costs, and use the Copy command on this formula for the other three years. In a similar manner, calculate all row totals for each of the column headings, a title, and perhaps some underlining and other decorative features to produce an attractive report of school expenditures.

2. Create a VP-Planner Plus worksheet that will list all of the courses you are taking this semester, along with the number of credit hours and the grade you expect. Also include a column showing the numerical equivalent for each grade you expect (A = 5.0, B = 4.0, C = 3.0, D = 2.0, and so on). Have your worksheet total your number of hours and your grade points, and calculate your grade point average.

3. Assume you've decided to purchase a new personal computer. List about eight or ten components and supplies you'll need (computer, display adapter, monitor, disk drives, expansion boards, printer, cables, diskettes, paper, and so on). Enter these headings into column A and budget an amount for each item in column B. Using ads from computer magazines or information from a local retailer, enter the actual costs for these items into column C. Enter a formula and use the Copy command to calculate the differences between your budgeted and actual costs in column D and the percent differences in column E. Also include column totals for each of the numeric columns, and add appropriate column and report headings.

4. Use VP-Planner Plus to generate a nice-looking calendar for this month. Each day should contain at least enough space to write a couple of lines of a few words each, so you can include appointments, holidays, birthdays, and so on. Enter appropriate headings and lines between all days and around the outside of the calendar.

5. At many popular fast food restaurants you are given a simple receipt when you purchase a meal. Get such a receipt, and then create a VP-Planner Plus worksheet that will produce a similar receipt after entering a typical customer's meal selections. Don't forget that there might be more than one of any item ordered, and don't forget to include a state sales tax.

6. Create a VP-Planner Plus worksheet that will display a compound interest table. Down column A, you should have the number of years, from 1 through 20. Across the top of your table, have columns for 5%, 5.25%, 5.5%, up to 7%. Compound interest tables are usually prepared for an initial investment of $1.00. Dress up your table with appropriate headings, lines, and a report title. Assume quarterly compounding, the formula for which is:

   V = P * (1 + R / C) ^ (N * C)

   where:
   V = value
   P = principal ($1.00 in this problem)
   R = interest rate (between 0.05 and 0.07)
   C = number of compoundings per year (4)
   N = number of years (20)
   * stands for multiplication
   ^ stands for exponentiation

   Utilize formulas and the Copy command as much as you can in your worksheet. As a check, the value of $1.00 at 7% for 20 years, compounded quarterly (which should appear in the lower-right corner of your worksheet), is slightly over $4.00.

7. In a small local newspaper the fee for classified advertising is a function of the price charged for the item. The fee is collected only if the item sells. The fee is 10% of the first $100.00 of the advertised price, plus 3% of the second $100.00, plus 2% of the third $100.00, plus 1% of the amount of the advertised price over $300.00. There is a minimum fee of $1.00 for any item sold. Create a VP-Planner Plus worksheet that will accept the advertised price as input and calculate the advertising fee. Test your worksheet with prices of $140.00 (fee = $11.20) and $750.00 (fee = $19.50).

8. Perhaps you heard the problem about the king and the checkerboard and the grains of wheat when you were a child. It seems that the king won great acclaim from his subjects by abolishing all taxes. In their place, he told the people that they would have to place one grain of wheat in one square of a checkerboard at the end of the first year. At the end of the second year, they would owe him two grains, placed in the second square. At the end of the third year, they would owe just four grains, placed in the third square, and at the end of the fourth year, just eight grains in the fourth square, and so on up to the sixty-fourth square of the checkerboard. After that, they would own their land outright and wouldn't have to give up any more wheat. Update this problem using pennies instead of wheat, and produce a VP-Planner Plus worksheet that shows each of the sixty-four years, the amount paid that year, and the total amount paid to date.

9. Assume you own 200 individual student apartments now renting for $110.00 a month. Since all your apartments are currently occupied, your gross is $22,000.00 per month. A real estate agent tells you your rent is way too low, but he further states that if you decide to raise the rent, you would lose one tenant for every $7.50 rent increase. In other words, you would be able to rent only 199 of the apartments at $117.50, 198 apartments at $125.00, and so on. Prepare a VP-Planner Plus worksheet that will list in one column the number of apartments rented, in the second column the rent per apartment, and in the third column the gross income for that particular combination of number rented and rent per apartment. What does your table suggest that rent should be? Document your

worksheet with headings, and use formulas and the Copy command wherever possible. Can you devise a way to get VP-Planner Plus to search the gross income column and identify the highest gross income, the number to rent, and the rent to charge?

10. Use VP-Planner Plus to duplicate the following table. Be sure to have your worksheet calculate all totals as well as the percent change figures with formulas.

Where the Jobs Are

Industry	**1978**	**1990**	**% Change**
Agriculture, forestry, and fisheries	269	600	102.4
Mining	3,176	6,300	123.0
Construction	2,481	4,500	98.4
Manufacturing	73,830	129,000	74.7
Transportation, public utilities, and communications	12,445	23,000	84.8
Wholesale, retail trade	19,409	35,000	80.3
Finance, insurance, and real estate	26,300	51,000	93.9
Services	84,366	204,000	141.8
Government	24,722	46,600	88.5
Total all industries	246,998	500,000	102.4

Source: U.S. Bureau of Labor Statistics

11. Some of the VP-Planner Plus problems presented in this manual may have surprised you because spreadsheets can apparently be used for many applications besides accounting. There are problems concerning calendars, word processing, probability, even games. What do you think about using VP-Planner Plus to draw flowcharts of computer programs? Can this be easily done? Try it for a simple flowchart, and describe your effort. What troubles did you encounter? What are the advantages and disadvantages of using VP-Planner Plus in such a manner?

12. The "average" American spends the following part of each after-tax dollar:

Items	**Part of Each Dollar**
Food, alcohol, and tobacco	22.3 cents
Housing	14.5
Household operation	14.4
Transportation	13.6
Clothing	10.1
Medical care	7.7
Recreation	6.5
Personal business	5.6
Private education	1.7
Personal care	1.5
Religious & welfare activities	1.4
Foreign travel	0.7

Use VP-Planner Plus to produce a report comparing your estimated expenses in each of these categories by adding columns for your expenses, the actual differences, and the percentage differences.

13. Balancing your checkbook is easy, if you use the form many banks put on the back of your monthly statement. Replicate the following form in a worksheet, so that you can use VP-Planner Plus to balance your checkbook.

CHECKS OUTSTANDING
(Written but not yet shown on this statement)

Check Number	Amount
Total	

ACCOUNT BALANCE (Shown this statement)	$ ______
ADD DEPOSITS (Made but not shown on this statement)	$ ______
TOTAL	$ ______
SUBTRACT CHECKS OUTSTANDING	$ ______
BALANCE (Should agree with your checkbook)	$ ______

14. Suppose you start a bank savings account that pays interest at a rate of 6% per year, and interest is paid monthly. You will receive 0.5% per month on your balance. You decide to begin a systematic savings plan in which you'll deposit $10.00 per month. Create a VP-Planner Plus worksheet that will display a table showing the amount of interest each month and the ending balance each month for a period of five years. Include appropriate formatting, headings, and a title. How would you have to modify your worksheet so that any yearly interest percentage and any monthly deposit could be entered?

15. Consider the categories of expenses for a typical traveling businessperson (airline tickets, automobile rental, mileage, meals, lodging, supplies, and so on). Construct a VP-Planner Plus worksheet that would allow one to accumulate his or her daily expenses for a week, total all rows and columns, and do a grand total.

16. Widen column A so that you can enter a dozen or so names, perhaps of fellow students. Enter Social Security numbers in column B, and in column C enter a numerical exam grade for each student. Use the print command to print this table. Now use the Worksheet Column Hide command on column A. Print the worksheet again. What happened to the names? Don't worry, they're not erased, merely hidden. VP-Planner Plus lets you hide sensitive data such as these names. To redisplay the names, execute the Worksheet Column Display command and enter column A for the range.

17. Create a VP-Planner Plus worksheet that will allow you to enter the amount of a purchase in a store (less than or equal to $1.00) in cell A1. Assume the customer always pays with a single dollar bill. Your worksheet should calculate the change to give the customer, putting the number of quarters to give in cell B1, the number of dimes in C1, the number of nickels in D1, and the number of pennies in E1. Of course, you'll want to minimize the number of coins given as change; in other words, don't give fifty pennies or ten nickels change for a $0.50 purchase.

18. The salvage value of an asset at the end of a given year can be determined by this formula:

S = P * (1 – i) ^ Y

where:	S = the salvage value	* stands for multiplication
	P = the original price	^ stands for exponentiation
	i = the depreciation rate	
	Y = the age in years	

For example, say your computer is three years old. You bought it for $895.00 and depreciate it at a rate of 15%. In this case the salvage value calculates to $549.64. Create a VP-Planner Plus worksheet to solve problems of this type.

19. Here's a recipe for strawberry shortcake, together with the conversion factors and some sample prices for the ingredients:

Strawberry Shortcake–serves 8		
3 cups flour	2.5 cups/lb.	$1.59 for 5 lbs.
3.25 tsp. baking powder	15 tsp./oz.	0.48 for 4 oz.
0.25 cup sugar	2 cups/lb.	1.19 for 5 lbs.
1.25 tsp. salt	6 tsp./oz.	0.27 for 1 lb.
0.5 cup butter	2 cups/lb.	1.29 for 1 lb.
1 egg	12/dozen	0.79 per dozen
2/3 cup milk	4 cups/qt.	0.59 per quart
3 pints strawberries		0.49 per pint
0.5 pint whipping cream		0.59 per 0.5 pint

Create a VP-Planner Plus worksheet that will calculate the cost of making the shortcake per this recipe, and also calculate the cost per serving. Your worksheet should allow you to change the prices for each of the items and recalculate the cost. How would you use your worksheet to calculate the cost per serving if you made the servings a little smaller and used the same cake to serve twelve people?

20. Data processing instructors have known for a long time the value of games in teaching computer programming. In fact, the easiest of games is often very difficult to simulate in a typical high-level programming language such as BASIC, FORTRAN, or Pascal. Games do, however, capture the interest of students, and they usually make excellent teaching tools. Consider the simple Tic-Tac-Toe game. Try to figure out how to simulate this game with a VP-Planner Plus worksheet. What problems do you encounter? Is it even possible?

Appendix

Software Installation

Most operating systems and application packages must be installed on your computer before you can use them. This typically involves running a special installation or setup program included with the software. Installation programs often create a new subdirectory on your hard disk, copy the files from the floppy disks included with the package to that subdirectory, and let you specify what kind of hardware you have. At most school microcomputer labs, this has already been done for you by the attendants. If you own a computer, however, you will probably have to install any new software you purchase yourself. The documentation that comes with the software should explain, step-by-step, how to run the installation program, and answer any questions that may be asked about your hardware and software. Let's briefly go over the steps necessary to install the software we discussed in this *Software Guide*: DOS and VP-Planner Plus.

MS- and PC-DOS Version 3.30

MS-DOS 3.30 and PC-DOS 3.30 are very similar. The MS-DOS package comes with two manuals entitled *MS-DOS User's Guide* and *MS-DOS User's Reference*. The first one contains the instructions for installing the system. The package can be purchased on either 3½-inch, 720K floppy disks, or 5¼-inch, 360K floppy disks. The 5¼-inch package comes with two disks, one labeled *Startup* and the other *Operating*.

Although the DOS 3.30 Startup diskette can be copied to another diskette to routinely boot up the computer from drive A, many people install the operating system on their hard disk C, if they have one. To install DOS 3.30 on a hard disk, follow these steps:

1. Insert the DOS 3.30 Startup disk into drive A.
2. Turn on the computer. If it is already on, press **Ctrl-Alt-Del** to reboot.
3. If the hard disk is not formatted (e.g., if you have a brand new computer), enter **format c: /s**. WARNING: Do not use this command if your hard disk is already formatted, or you will lose all files stored on it.
4. If the hard disk is already formatted with a previous version of DOS, enter **sys c:** instead of using the format command.
5. Enter **copy command.com c:** to copy the command processor to the hard disk.

6. If a subdirectory named DOS already exists on the hard disk, enter **del c:\dos*.*** to delete its contents. If such a subdirectory does not exist, enter **md c:\dos** to create it.
7. Enter **copy *.* c:\dos** to copy all the files from the Startup diskette to the DOS subdirectory on the hard disk.
8. Take the Startup diskette out of drive A, replace it with the Operating diskette, press **F3**, and press **Enter** to repeat the previous command and copy all of the files from the Operating diskette to the DOS subdirectory on the hard disk.
9. Remove the diskette from drive A, store all your original DOS diskettes in a safe place, and press **Ctrl-Alt-Del** to reboot your computer from the hard disk with DOS 3.30.
10. Enter **path c:\;c:\dos;** to set up the search paths for the root directory and the DOS subdirectory. You can add other search paths on the end of this command if you like. Ideally, this path command should be put in your AUTOEXEC.BAT file (see Chapter 2, Lesson 18).

IBM DOS Version 4.00

The DOS 4.00 package comes with two short manuals entitled *Getting Started with Disk Operating System Version 4.00* and *Using Disk Operating System Version 4.00*. The first one contains the instructions for installing the system. The package can be purchased on either 3½-inch, 720K floppy disks or 5¼-inch, 360K floppy disks. You should get the package with disks that match your floppy drive A. The 3½-inch package comes with two disks, one labeled *Install* and the other *Operating*. The 5¼-inch package comes with five disks labeled *Install, Select, Operating 1, Operating 2*, and *Operating 3*.

Although DOS 4.00 can be installed on floppy disks to boot up the computer from drive A, most people install the operating system on their hard disk C, if they have one. To install DOS 4.00 on a hard disk, follow these steps:

1. Insert the DOS 4.00 Install disk into drive A.
2. Turn on the computer. If it is already on, press **Ctrl-Alt-Del** to reboot.
3. After the copyright screen appears, press **Enter** and follow the instructions given by the installation program, which is called Select.
4. When you are finished with the installation program, remove the DOS floppy disk from drive A, store all your DOS disks in a safe place, and press **Ctrl-Alt-Del** to reboot your computer from the hard disk with DOS 4.00.

VP-Planner Plus Version 2.0

When you purchase VP-Planner Plus Version 2.0, you get a thick softcover manual and two 5¼-inch diskettes entitled *Program Disk* and *Sample Files*.

To install VP-Planner Plus on a hard disk, follow these steps:

1. Turn on your computer and boot up DOS.
2. Type **md \vpp** and press **Enter** to create a new subdirectory named VPP on your hard disk.

3. Type **cd \vpp** and press **Enter** to switch to the subdirectory you've just created.
4. Insert the Program Disk into drive A.
5. Type **copy a:*.*** and press **Enter**.
6. After the contents of the floppy disk have been copied into the VPP subdirectory, remove the disk from drive A.
7. Repeat steps 4 through 6 for the Sample Files diskette.
8. Put your original VP-Planner Plus floppy disks away in a safe place.

Glossary

adapter (also called an **expansion card**) a circuit board that connects a microcomputer to some external input or output device.

application package a program that enables a computer to accomplish useful tasks.

archive attribute a file attribute that is turned on when the file has been changed since the last time it was backed up.

ASCII American Standard Code for Information Interchange; the code used by most microcomputers for storing text in binary form.

auto-hyphenation a feature of some word processors that hyphenates words in a document when necessary; these hyphens may disappear if the document is reformatted.

bit the basic unit of data processing; 0 or 1, off or on.

block any section of text, from a single character to a whole document, that can be marked and treated as a single entity.

boot up to load the operating system into a computer's primary memory and begin its execution.

browse to skim through the records of a data base.

bug an error or problem in a computer program.

bus a set of wires and connectors that links the CPU to memory and other computer components.

byte a contiguous group of eight bits; the amount of memory it takes to store a single character.

cell the unit formed by the intersection of one row and one column in a spreadsheet.

cell pointer in a spreadsheet program, the highlighted bar that marks your current location in a spreadsheet.

character any single letter, number, punctuation mark, or symbol. It is important to note that the computer interprets spaces as characters also.

chip see *integrated circuit chip*.

code page a conversion table that tells DOS how to translate data stored as numeric values into letters, numbers, punctuation, and other symbols to be displayed or printed.

color graphics monitor a monitor that can display both text and graphics in more than one color.

command processor the program in an operating system that translates and acts on the commands entered by the user.

computer an electronic device that performs calculations and processes data into information.

control panel lines at the top or bottom of the screen used to display information, messages, menu choices, and prompts.

CPU central processing unit; the part of a computer that performs control operations, calculations, and logic.

cursor a small, blinking underscore or box that marks the position where characters appear on the screen when typed.

cut and paste the process of marking a block of text and moving it from one location in a document file to another location.

daisy-wheel printer a printer with solid, raised characters embossed on the ends of little arms arranged like the spokes of a wheel; for producing slow, but letter-quality output.

data numbers, text, pictures, sounds that are to be processed into information.

data base an organized collection of one or more files of related data.

data base management package software that lets you create, add to, delete from, update, rearrange, select from, print out, and otherwise administer data files such as mailing lists and inventories.

debug to remove the bugs from an imperfect computer program.

default the predefined settings for certain features (margins, line spacing, column widths, etc.) that a software package uses automatically when alternate settings have not been explicitly established.

delete to remove, erase, or destroy one or more pieces of information.

desk accessory a utility program that provides commonly used desk functions such as a calculator, calendar, or address book.

desktop publishing the use of a computer and laser printer to produce near-typeset quality documents.

device controller a set of chips or a circuit board that operates a piece of computer equipment such as a disk drive, display, keyboard, mouse, or printer.

device driver a file in an operating system that contains the programming code needed to attach and use some special devices.

directory a list of the files stored on a disk; another term for subdirectory.

disk a medium, consisting of one or more flat surfaces on which bits are usually recorded magnetically, used by computers to store information.

disk buffer an area of memory that DOS uses to temporarily hold data being read from or written to a disk.

disk drive a computer system component that reads and writes programs and data on disks.

diskette a floppy disk.

display output screen on which the computer presents text and graphic images; monitor.

display adapter a circuit board or set of chips that controls a monitor.

document the paper output of a word processor.

documentation the user manual or technical information about a computer or software package.

document file a collection of text created by a word processing program in such a way that the text includes embedded formatting codes.

DOS disk operating system; an operating system that is stored on a disk.

DOS shell a program that enhances PC-DOS or MS-DOS.

dot-matrix printer a common type of printer that constructs character images by repeatedly striking pins against the ribbon and paper.

draft mode the fastest print mode, in which low-quality characters are formed by a single pass of the printhead.

edit to make changes to a file.

expansion board a circuit board that plugs into an expansion slot.

expansion slot an internal connector that extends a computer's bus and accepts an additional circuit board.

expert system a computer program that contains a collection of facts and a list of rules for making inferences about those facts.

export to produce a file with one software package that is ultimately to be used by some other software package.

field a group of related characters in a data base record.

file a collection of information stored on a disk and loaded into primary memory when needed by a program; in a data base, a group of related records.

file attribute a characteristic of a DOS file such as *read-only* or *archived*.

file locking a feature of DOS that allows only one person to use a file or part of a file at a time.

file sharing a feature of DOS that allows two or more people to use the same file at the same time.

filter a program that accepts data as input, processes them in some way, then outputs them in a different form.

floppy disk an inexpensive, flexible magnetic medium for storing computer programs and data.

floppy disk drive a disk drive that accepts floppy disks.

formula in a spreadsheet, an expression that performs some calculations and is stored in a cell.

function in a spreadsheet, a predefined formula that lets you perform a useful operation with a minimum of typing.

function keys on an IBM-compatible computer, the keys on the left side or top of the keyboard labeled F1 through F10 or F12. Such keys are usually used to perform common operations with different software packages.

global pertaining to or acting upon an entire document, spreadsheet, or data base file.

graphics any kind of graphs, plots, drawings, and other images not restricted to text characters.

hard disk a high-capacity, completely-enclosed, rigid magnetic medium for storing computer programs and data.

hard disk drive a disk drive that contains one or more hard disks.

hard hyphen a hyphen inserted into a document by the user that remains in the document even after it has been reformatted.

hard page break a division between two pages in a document, manually generated by the user, that remains in the document even after it has been reformatted.

hard return a new line or paragraph in a document, manually generated by the user, that remains in the document even after it has been reformatted.

hard spaces spaces in a document, manually inserted by the user, that remain even after the document has been reformatted.

hardware the physical components of a computer system.

hypertext software that lets you store and retrieve all kinds of information in a nonsequential manner.

IBM-compatible any computer that works like a comparable IBM model and can run the same software.

import to use a file in one software package that was originally produced in another software package.

incremental backup the process of backing up only those files that have been added or modified since the last backup.

index to arrange a list of record numbers in some particular order.

information a more organized and useful form of input data.

ink-jet printer a printer with a mechanism for squirting tiny droplets of ink to form text and graphics on paper.

input any data or information entered into a computer.

integrated circuit chip a thin slice of semiconductor material, such as pure silicon crystal, impregnated with carefully selected impurities; commonly used in computers and many other electronic devices.

integrated software a package that combines word processing, spreadsheet, data base management, communications, and graphics applications.

K the abbreviation for kilobyte; 1K = 1024 bytes.

key a field used to sort or index the records of a data base.

keyboard the device with which you type input into the computer.

label in an operating system, a word that marks the place in a batch file where a GOTO command is to branch to.

label in a spreadsheet, a text entry in a cell.

label-prefix character in a spreadsheet, a symbol that explicitly indicates that the succeeding text is to be treated as a label.

laser printer a high-quality printer that uses tightly-focused beams of light to transfer images to paper.

letter-quality like the output of a good electric typewriter.

load to copy a program or data file from disk into memory.

local area network (LAN) a system in which several microcomputers are connected together so that they can share hardware, software, and data.

M the abbreviation for megabyte; 1M = 1,048,576 bytes.

macro a sequence of keystrokes that can be entered, named, and replayed.

magnetic disk a semi-permanent storage medium that can be erased and written over and over again.

memory the part of the computer that stores programs and data temporarily.

menu a list of options available in a program.

microcomputer a small computer that uses a single microprocessor chip as its central processing unit.

microprocessor a central processing unit made up of a single integrated circuit chip.

modem *mo*dulator-*dem*odulator; a device that enables a computer to transmit and receive programs and data over ordinary phone lines.

monitor a computer display screen.

monochrome graphics monitor a single-color screen that can display both text and graphics.

monochrome text monitor a single-color screen that displays sharply-defined characters, but no graphics.

motherboard the main circuit board of a computer.

mouse an input device consisting of a small box with one or more buttons that is slid across the table top and allows the user to manipulate objects on the screen and select menu options.

NLQ near letter quality; a dot-matrix print mode that produces attractive output by having the printhead make two or more passes over each character.

numeric keypad on an IBM-compatible computer, the area on the right side of the keyboard arranged like the number keys on a calculator.

on-line connected to and controlled by the computer.

on-line reference a program such as a spelling checker, thesaurus, or user manual that you can use while running another program.

operating system the software that controls and supports a computer system's hardware.

output any information produced by the computer; the computer's responses to a user's input.

page break a location in a document file where a new page is to begin.

page layout software a program that lets you combine the output of a word processor and graphics program to produce documents on a laser printer.

partition a section of a hard disk that contains an operating system.

personal computer a microcomputer.

piping a feature of DOS, symbolized by the | (vertical bar), that allows the user to take the output of one command that would normally go to the display screen and feed it as input to another command.

pixel picture element; a tiny dot on a computer display.

primary memory where a computer stores the programs and data it is currently using.

printer a device for producing computer output on paper.

program a sequence of step-by-step instructions that run a computer.

programmer a person who creates computer programs.

programming language a set of symbols and rules to direct the operations of a computer.

project management package software to help you formally plan and control a complex undertaking.

prompt a symbol or statement that indicates the computer is waiting for a response from the user.

RAM Random Access Memory; the portion of a computer's primary memory used to store programs and data temporarily; also known as read/write memory.

range in a spreadsheet, a designation of contiguous cells.

read-only attribute a file attribute that, when turned on, prevents a file from being changed or deleted.

record a set of related fields in a data base.

redirection a feature of DOS, symbolized by >, <, >>, that allows you to send the output of a command to some other program or output device.

relational data base a data base that is organized in two-dimensional tables of rows (records) and columns (fields).

replaceable parameter a feature of DOS that allows the user to pass information to a batch file while it is running.

resolution the sharpness of a display screen.

right justification aligning text to the right margin.

ROM Read Only Memory; permanent primary storage that is encoded with programs and data at the factory, and can be read and used, but never erased, changed, or augmented, by the user.

scroll to shift what is on a computer display screen so that other areas are visible.

soft page break a division between two pages in a document that is automatically generated by a word processor; may be changed if the document is reformatted.

soft return a new line or paragraph in a document that is automatically generated by a word processor; may be changed if the document is reformatted.

soft spaces spaces between words in a document that are generated by a word processor to justify text in a document; may be changed if the document is reformatted.

software a program or set of programs that tells a computer system what to do.

software integration the sharing of data files between different software packages.

sort to arrange the records of a data base in some particular order.

spreadsheet a table of columns and rows of numbers, text labels, and formulas used in an electronic spreadsheet package for the manipulation of numerical, financial, and accounting data.

spreadsheet package software that lets you manipulate spreadsheets.

system board the main circuit board of a computer.

system software the software that handles the many details of managing a computer system.

system unit in IBM-compatible computers, the box that contains the central processing unit, memory, circuit boards, disk drives, and power switch for the system.

upwardly compatible an operating system or software package that adds new capabilities, yet retains all previous features.

utility a small, specific program that adds handy features to a particular operating system or application package.

windowing environment software that allows you to divide your screen into two or more boxes and run a separate program in each one.

word processing package a software package used to create, enter, edit, format, store, and print documents.

word wrap a word processing feature that automatically begins new lines when necessary without the user having to press the Enter key (carriage return).

Answers to Exercises

Chapter 1 The Microcomputer

Multiple Choice

1. c	6. c	11. a	16. c
2. a	7. c	12. b	17. d
3. d	8. b	13. a	18. c
4. b	9. a	14. b	19. b
5. a	10. d	15. d	20. c

Fill-In

1. IBM-compatible
2. processing
3. hardware
4. bus
5. RAM, ROM
6. hard disk drives
7. pixels
8. VGA
9. mouse
10. cursor
11. dot-matrix
12. software
13. languages
14. application
15. graphics
16. desktop publishing or page layout
17. integrated
18. windowing
19. project
20. expert

Chapter 2 The PC-DOS Operating System

Multiple Choice

1. c	6. a	11. d	16. a
2. b	7. c	12. b	17. b
3. a	8. c	13. c	18. d
4. d	9. b	14. d	19. c
5. d	10. a	15. b	20. a

Fill-In

1. files
2. PC-DOS, MS-DOS
3. memory
4. date, time
5. DIR
6. eight
7. classify
8. Escape or Esc
9. Ctrl-Break
10. prompt
11. CHKDSK
12. formatted
13. COPY
14. global
15. format
16. rename
17. ERASE or DEL
18. text
19. PRINT
20. MD or MKDIR, CD or CHDIR, RD or RMDIR

Chapter 3 VP-Planner Plus

Multiple Choice

1. c	6. b	11. b	16. a
2. c	7. d	12. c	17. c
3. d	8. a	13. a	18. c
4. a	9. b	14. d	19. a
5. b	10. c	15. b	20. d

Fill-In

1. rows, columns
2. cell
3. two
4. control panel
5. arrow keys
6. Home
7. numbers, labels, formulas
8. EDIT
9. / (forward slash)
10. Enter
11. range
12. Move
13. File Combine
14. help
15. Save
16. Retrieve
17. Logical
18. functions
19. Alt
20. /gp or Graphics Print